THE MANX ELECTRIC

INTRODUCTION

The Manx Electric Railway is unique in many ways. It is the longest electric tramway operating in the British Isles and has continued in operation since the pioneering days of last century. Two of the cars are the oldest tramcars operating regularly anywhere in the world. In addition, the Snaefell Mountain Railway is the only one of its kind in Britain. The fact that the coastal and mountain railways remain virtually intact, with much of the rolling stock in its original form, is a tribute to the founders of the railways, the engineers and inventors of a past age, the directors and staff of the Manx Electric Railway Company and, in more recent years, the declared intention of the Manx people, through Tynwald, to preserve a cherished part of their inheritance.

Today the railways are an important part of railway heritage which attract enthusiasts from many parts of the world. For the majority of visitors to the Isle of Man it is an opportunity to travel back into history along routes traversed by many millions of people as they experienced some of the most delightful and spectacular scenery to be found anywhere. The traditional friendly welcome remains, as do the dedicated skills of the maintenance staff handed down through many generations. The great majority of visitors regard their visit to the Island incomplete without a ride on the Manx Electric Railway, and in so doing are playing their part in its preservation.

Robert Smith B.A., M.C.I.T.
Tramsport Executive.

A PIONEER OF ELECTRIC RAILWAYS

When steam railways were just about connecting every town and village throughout Britain, a new form of traction was demonstrated at the Berlin Trades Fair of 1879. It was the work of Werner von Siemens who had harnessed electro-magnetic forces to provide mechanical locomotive power. Its practical application was developed on short lines both in Britain and America where the 'street car' was seen as the means of providing transport in cities where steam railways were not practicable. Later, these electric tramways were extended to connect cities. In Britain, developments were hesitant though rival Blackpool introduced its first electric trams along the sea front as early as 1885. On the other hand it was not until the beginning of the century that London and Birmingham began replacing the ubiquitous horse-buses with electric trams.

However, there was one place in the British Isles where electro-motive power was to be applied with considerable entrepreneurial zeal; that was in the Isle of Man. There was a need to provide transport for a part of the Island where the gradients deterred a steam railway. Could an electric railway be the answer? This was provided in 1893 with resounding success. It borrowed heavily from the American inter urban idea but would here be used to connect more isolated parts of the Island. The undertaking aroused great interest and it became a pioneer for city transport which became a mark of civic pride throughout Britain. Electric trams have long since given way to motorised transport but the Manx Electric Railway survives as a permanent reminder of the days when 'taking a tram' was part of everyday life. It can also claim to be a progenitor of the hi-speed intercity rail links of today.

The front cover shows the world's oldest operational electric tramcar on the climb to Howstrake from Groudle .

MEN OF ENTERPRISE

By the end of the 1880's the Isle of Man, and Douglas in particular, was gripped by the booming tourist industry which would project the Island into the twentieth century. The sweep of Douglas Bay was rapidly being lined with hotels offering the best of accommodation, including gas illumination. Behind the sea front the banks of fields were awaiting the rows of boarding houses which would be needed to accommodate the number of visitors steadily growing towards half a million a year. The Isle of Man was rapidly becoming the 'Playground of the North' and the mill and factory workers, having gained paid holidays, flocked to the Island for their annual visit. For their entertainment there was a range of theatres and ballrooms while in daytime they could explore the many beauty spots now made accessible by the Isle of Man Steam Railway. The line to Peel was opened in 1873 and Port Erin was reached the following year. Ramsey had to wait until 1879 with a line travelling along the west coast to join the Douglas-Peel railway at St. John's. However, this left one part of the Island with only limited access – the picturesque north east coast. Boat trips were available with stops at Laxey, Dhoon and Ramsey. Also available were trips by horse-drawn carriages which required passengers to alight for the steep hills. But for the great majority wishing to visit the now famous Laxey Wheel and the mine workings, a day's outing on foot was required. The idea of a steam railway to these parts was mooted more than once and, for example, the Douglas, Laxey and Ramsey Railway Company was formed in 1882 with plans to branch from the Peel line at Quarterbridge and climb northwards to Onchan and thence to Laxey. But these schemes, frought with many engineering difficulties and steep gradients, came to nought. It was a challenge waiting for history to happen.

Alexander Bruce, railway visionary, Manager of the Dumbell Banking Company and Chairman of the Isle of Man Tramways and Electric Power Company.

Among the many remarkable characters in the forefront of developments on the Island at that time was Mr Alexander Bruce. He had started his career with the City of Glasgow Bank and came to the Island to manage its subsiduary, the Bank of Mona. The disastrous collapse of the City of Glasgow Bank in 1878 saw Bruce move to another local bank, the Dumbell Banking Company Ltd. which was also in a parlous state. However, by dint of hard work and a certain amount of good luck Mr Bruce led the bank into years of prosperity lasting for the rest of the century. A man of enterprise he teamed up with a civil engineer, Mr Frederick Saunderson. The engineer had come from Ireland in 1865 and had connections with the family of the famous Captain Rowe of the Great Laxey Mine. With railway engineering in Ireland behind him he turned his attention to real estate promotion and was in charge of the South Ramsey Estate in the late 1880's. Together, Bruce and Saunderson turned their attention to the large Howstrake estate to the north of Douglas, mainly rough grazing land which rose from the steep cliffs to a height of 427 feet on Banks Howe. They had visions of large scale housing developments and pleasure grounds in mind.

Plans for the development were drawn up in 1889 and final approval was granted in 1892 by Tynwald, the Manx Parliament, for the Howstrake estate to be purchased in the name of Mr Saunderson. He was backed by Mr Alfred Jones Lusty, a wealthy London merchant who had retired to the Island and had actually lived on the estate. Approval was conditional upon a road, with ancillary services, being built adjacent to the coast to give access to the new properties. To

Port e Vada Creek was filled in to provide a site for the Derby Castle Depot in 1893, the same year the Derby Castle Theatre on the right was being completed. Work on the track and roadway is in progress while, beyond Strathallan Crescent, can be seen the horse-car shed at the foot of Burnt Mill Hill, now Summerhill.

connect this new road with the north end of the Strathallan Crescent promenade it was necessary to construct a sea wall across Port y Vada creek which would enable the land behind to be reclaimed. Approval was given but now the road was to be accompanied by a tramway (single or double track) 'to be operated by animal, steam, electric or any other power.' With the legal requirements settled the way was clear to construct a road and railway as far as the extremity of the Howstrake estate above Groudle. The owner of the next estate, Bibaloe, was Mr R. M. Broadbent who was planning the construction of a hotel along with making the untouched Groudle Glen a beauty spot with rustic bridges, footpaths etc for the delight of holidaymakers. Little time was lost in obtaining the necessary land to bring the railway to the site of the hotel and glen entrance.

The men of enterprise – Bruce, Saunderson, Lusty and their associates – now formed themselves into the DOUGLAS BAY ESTATE LTD. which was registered in September, 1892, with a capital of £50,000. Saunderson's rights and the Howstrake estate were taken over with the declared intent of constructing a tramway and public road as far as Groudle, and the erection of electric plant on the reclaimed land behind the sea wall at Port e Vada. Mr Bruce, a man of many enterprises and held in the highest regard, was now Treasurer of Douglas town and a J.P. He could see the great potential of an electric railway and had made it his business to seek the best advice. He was referred to Dr Edward Hopkinson, a partner in Mather and Platt of the Salford Ironworks. Dr Hopkinson was also associated with the Chloride Electrical Storage Syndicate and had gained experience in electric traction while working on the City and South London Railway. Sir William Mather had obtained the British rights of the Edison dynamo from which Dr Edward's brother, Dr John Hopkinson, had developed the Edison-

Hopkinson dynamo (later the 'Manchester' dynamo) which Mather and Platt began to manufacture.

Work on laying the 2½ mile track began in earnest early in 1893. Where necessary the rock face was blasted to level the ground to take the track and the accompanying roadway, though little attention was paid to the latter other than keeping it level with the track and separating it by a line of stones. The rails arrived in May, sufficient for a single line which was laid on the seaward side of the track leaving room for the twin line to be laid on the inside. The gauge adopted was that of 3 feet which the Isle of Man Railway had already decided was ideal for its passenger traffic. The rails were of 56 lb per yard and were affixed to sleepers of scotch fir or larch positioned on an earth ballast. Poles were erected on the central position to serve the twin line, but with single bracket arms to suspend the conductor wire. Each pole was decorated with an ornamental collar though these have long since disappeared.

The stone wall at Port e Vada was the first part of the construction work and the creek, once favoured by boys going for a 'dip,' had been filled in and levelled to take the road originally planned and now accompanied by the rail track from the terminus. Behind this was ample space for the depot buildings constructed in one block. Largest was the car depot with three tracks and giving shelter for nine cars or trailers. Each track was equipped with inspection pits. The depot was of wooden construction with a corrugated iron roof, as was the adjoining workshop. Next was the stone built building of the engine and boiler houses, the latter having a chimney of 60 feet. The depot took its name from Derby Castle, a private dwelling from the early part of last century. Its spacious grounds were taken over for the famous ballroom and theatre which was being built at the same time as the railway. The site is now occupied by the Summerland leisure centre but 'Derby Castle' lives on as the name of the railway's Douglas terminus and depot.

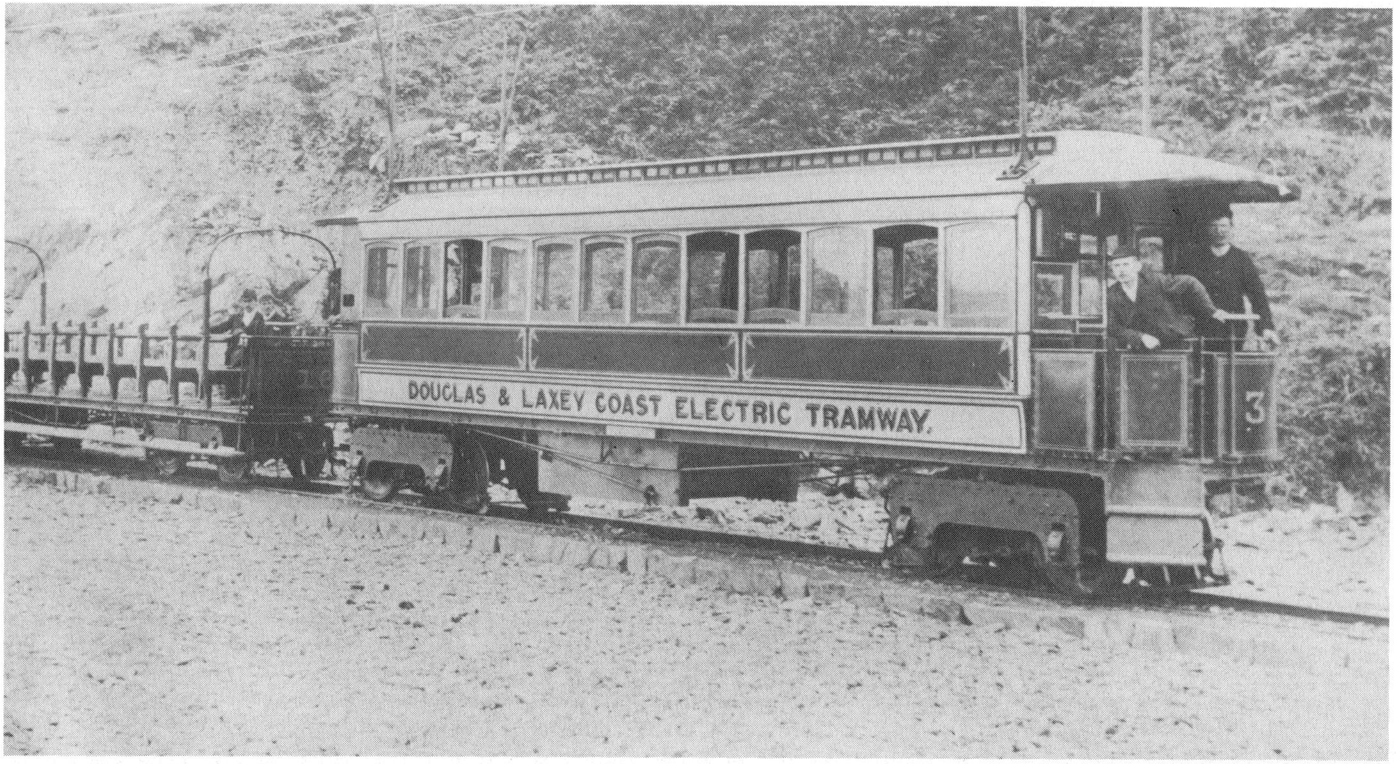

Engineers and officials on a trial run on the single line to Groudle prior to the first passenger service which opened on 7th September, 1893.

The boiler house contained two large Galloway boilers to supply steam for the two 90 hp Galloway marine engines positioned in the engine house. The engines had flywheels of 9 feet diameter which were linked by leather belts to two of the Mather and Platt 'Manchester' type dynamos They could give an output of 100 amps at 500 volts DC which had been decided upon as the required current for operating the motor cars. By the beginning of August three saloon cars and six open trailers had been delivered by G. F. Milnes and Co. of Birkenhead. The firm had long been associated with horse trams but were also building cable and steam track cars. For the new venture of electric tramcars they looked to American designs as evidenced in the rolling stock delivered to Douglas. The cars were equipped with rigid bow collectors at either end of the cars to pick up current from the overhead conductor wire. These were new and were to suffer teething problems which delayed the start of operations, the first car not reaching Groudle until August 26th. This was followed by all three cars being brought into use with free rides for the public who had been patiently waiting for the new experience.

On September 7th the regular service was inaugurated and continued until closing for the winter on September 28th. During the 17 days of the service over 20,000 passengers had been carried at the minimum 3d. fare. They marvelled at the way the cars took them up the 1 in 24 gradient past Onchan Head and then gathered speed culminating in the exhilarating descent to Groudle where the 1 in 24 gradient was repeated. A gradual stop brought them outside the Groudle Hotel which had been anticipating the arrival of the cars since July. Everyone agreed that the enterprise was a great success which, no doubt, must have brought great satisfaction to Mr Bruce and his fellow directors.

The Groudle Hotel and Glen were ready to receive the first of many millions of visitors in July, 1893, the first trams arriving in September. Note the loop for the single line.

PRESSING ON TO LAXEY

As far as Alexander Bruce was concerned the tramway to Groudle was but a proving ground for something more ambitious - he had visions of Laxey being reached as soon as practicable. In March, 1893, six months before the Groudle service began, steps were being taken to gain Tynwald approval for the extension. Saunderson had already planned the route for track and road as far as Baldromma Beg where it met the Douglas to Laxey road, close to the Half Way House (Liverpool Arms). The land was now owned by the DOUGLAS BAY ESTATE AND GROUDLE GLEN COMPANY LTD. A new operating company, THE DOUGLAS AND LAXEY COAST ELECTRIC TRAMWAY COMPANY, was launched with an authorised capital of £50,000, with a view to operating a tramway between Douglas and Laxey. The capital came from the original Howstrake company as the subscribers were largely the same. This new company would take over the land as far as Baldromma Beg on completion of the tramway, leaving the Douglas Bay Estate Company to develop Howstrake Park (Howstrake Holiday Camp) and an 18 hole golf course.

Final Tynwald approval for the extension was granted in November with certain conditions. The maximum gradient was to be 1 in 20 and speeds restricted to 8 mph where track and road ran together, and 6 mph at cross roads. Fencing was required where track and road were on different levels. There should be government inspection before public use of the extension. A charge of 2d a mile was permitted with a 3d minimum fare. Each passenger should be allowed to carry up to 28lb free of charge. There would be no third class fare, it being pointed out by Saunderson that all carriages would be first class and 'exceedingly well got up!' Government also insisted that freight and mail should be carried at a fixed rate when it was realised that any chance of a steam railway was now out of the question. The Tynwald Act gave compulsory purchase powers to acquire land along the approved route.

Construction was resumed in February, 1894, with the laying of the second line to Groudle which opened at the end of May and by July this section was carrying about 8,000

In the new Derby Castle Depot staff proudly pose in 1894 beside trams ready for the opening of the route to Laxey.

passengers a week. Meanwhile an impressive viaduct with three 20 feet spans was being built to take track and road over the Groudle river. (The large rustic Groudle station opposite the hotel was added the following year). The line then progressed as planned to the Laxey terminus short of the Rencell road. Nowhere was a gradient of more than 1 in 25 required. At Laxey, a station was built to which a car depot was added at a later date. At Derby Castle a further shed for eight cars or trailers was added.

The extension of the line to over 6½ miles needed additional traction current so a third boiler, engine and a more efficient Hopkinson generator were installed at Derby Castle depot. An underground feeder line supplied power to points as far as the Half Way House. The staff at Derby Castle was increased to include a smith, two station foremen, a fitter, two carpenters, an engine driver and fireman, general hands and several switchgear men. There were also eight apprentices taken on; many of this staff were to give a lifetime of service to the railway. At Laxey a new power station was built close to the river at the bottom of the slope below the line. Two generators of the newer type provided power which was supplied to two points on the Laxey ascent. The feeder points meant that the entire line was divided into six electrical sections.

As a back-up supply of electrical power a wooden battery house was positioned at Groudle between the station and bridge. This was initially equipped with 240 cells made by the Chloride Electric Storage Syndicate and which were capable of being discharged at the rate of 140 amps at 500 volts amps for three hours. The batteries were charged once or twice a week and the discharge was available when necessary, such as two overloaded cars making an uphill start at the same time. This idea was entirely new and was to be adopted by other early tramways. In 1899 the batteries were changed to Chloride R type with a 50% higher discharge rate. However, such a system was soon to become obsolescent but it survived at Groudle until 1944, the Manx Electric and Mersey Railways being the last of the British traction examples.

The construction and mode of operating the extended line to Laxey caused considerable interest both in Britain and the United States. Here new frontiers were being explored to cover distance and gradients; such heavy electrical engineering had not been seen before while the generating

Horse, steam and electric power together at Port Jack in 1894 when the twin track to Groudle was completed. The Douglas Bay Hotel was the first to be illuminated by electricity supplied from the Derby Castle Power Station. Nearly a hundred years later the famous hotel was demolished.

plant and the feeder system was looked upon as important new ventures for the British electrical engineering industry. Aware of this Tynwald insisted that everything should be thoroughly inspected before public use. For the engineering aspects Colonel Rich was called upon. Latterly he had been senior inspector of railways to the Board of Trade and had visited the Island for a similar purpose in 1873 and 1874 to approve the new lines of the Isle of Man Railway. Colonel Rich expressed his approval with the proviso that pointsmen with flags (lamps at night) should be positioned at the termini. He also wanted protective guards at either side of road crossings and warning notices against the danger of touching the overhead wires. For the electrical engineering Major Cardew gave his approval though he expressed his concern about the high voltage available, much higher than in other parts of Britain, though common in America.

As regards rolling stock six more saloon cars were supplied by Milnes and numbered 4 - 9. They were of an improved design to the first three, having platform vestibules. All had longitudinal seats for 36 passengers. Again Mather and Platt provided the electric motors and equipment. All nine cars now had the improved type of bow collector of which Dr Edward Hopkinson had patented the springing now applied to his brother's rigid type. The effect was to give a greater height range and flexibility. It still left the wire at each supporting pole but one bow was always in contact. Six new trailers were also purchased.

The inspections took place on Friday, 27th July, 1894, and the formal opening took place the following afternoon. Just about all of Laxey, including many of the miners and their families, turned out for this great occasion. When the special car arrived with the officials the combined Laxey and Laxey Temperance bands struck up with 'See the conquering hero comes.' Alexander Bruce was very much the hero and there was also much praise (and cheers) for Mr Saunderson, Dr Hopkinson and his assistants including Joshua Shaw of Barnard and Callender's who was the overhead specialist. The new electric tramway was to put Laxey well and truly on the map. Though the mines were beginning to wane, Lady Isabella, the Great Wheel, was to keep turning for many more years and was now visited by thousands daily. Already the Laxey Glen Gardens were being developed as a major attraction so Laxey could look forward to benefiting

Directors and officials pose at Groudle on their way to the official opening of the line to Laxey on 28th July 1894.

from the part it was now ready to play in the tourist industry. And there was more to come!

Although the six new saloon cars bore the name 'Douglas and Laxey Electric Tramway,' events were moving fast and the company had already changed its name in April of that year following the purchase and take-over of the Douglas horse trams. It was in 1876 that Mr Thomas Lightfoot had conceived the idea of this form of transport being provided for the benefit of visitors. The first trams ran in August 1876 along the northern part of the sea front and the following year the line was extended over the new Loch Promenade as far as Victoria Pier, thus providing a convenient form of transport for the arrivals by steamer to reach their hotels. The trams proved immensely popular and Mr Lightfoot sold his enterprise in 1882 to a local consortium, The Isle of Man Tramway Ltd., for about £15,000. The system was expanded annually to meet the demand and by 1893 it had a fleet of 29 cars which, during the year, had carried over 900,000 passengers. After complex negotiations the concern was sold for £38,000 to the Douglas and Laxey Coast Electric Tramway Company which then changed its name to ISLE OF MAN TRAMWAYS AND ELECTRIC POWER COMPANY LIMITED. The Douglas Town Commissioners, who had first option on the horse trams, only agreed to such a change provided that the new company should build and operate a tramway for the benefit of residents in the growing part of Upper Douglas. Thus the Upper Douglas Cable Tramway was duly built and opened in 1896.

It was the declared aim of Mr Bruce that the horse trams should be replaced by new electric cars, with overhead wires, thus making Victoria Pier an ideal terminus for his system. Many inducements were presented to the Town Commissioners including an offer to light free of charge all the promenades and much of Upper Douglas in return for selling current in Douglas to private consumers. Whilst the committee set up to consider these proposals was in favour there were many objectors, notably the hoteliers and operators of horse carriages. Douglas gained Borough status in 1896 and, following fresh elections, the scheme was withdrawn by the promoters. The company's intention to provide electricity for public consumption, however, met with some success and its first customer was the brand new Douglas Bay Hotel (recently demolished) with some 250 lamps. In 1896 new equipment was hired from Mather and Platt and by 1900 3,190 lamps were being supplied to private houses and the Derby Castle Opera House. Parts of Onchan village was also supplied, using 15 amp arc-lamps, thus making the village the first to change from gas to electric street lighting.

Laxey Station as it was in 1894-5 before being moved closer to the village by bridging Rencell Hill

CHALLENGE OF SNAEFELL

Rising to 2,036 feet above sea level Snaefell (Scandinavian for Snow Mountain) is the Island's highest point and the only 'true' Manx mountain. On a clear day, the visitor to its majestic sunmmit is rewarded by panoramic views of the Island and across the Irish Sea to England, Wales, Scotland and Ireland. For early visitors to the summit, it meant a climb either on foot or on horseback. For a small fee the views could be observed through a telescope erected by a local entrepreneur. For Mr Bruce and company it was an experience which should be shared not by a few, but by thousands!

It is not surprising, therefore, that the Isle of Man Tramways and Electric Power Company, having reached Laxey, should announce at the end of 1894 plans to build an electric tramway to the summit of Snaefell, undeterred by the fact that a mountain railway, either steam or electric, had not been attempted in Britain before. Amazingly, the entire tramway was opened on 21st August just seven months after work commenced.

Mr Bruce and his fellow directors were joined by others who formed a SNAEFELL MOUNTAIN RAILWAY ASSOCIATION to build the line. George Noble Fell was appointed to supervise the construction work and Dr Edward Hopkinson to supervise the electrical work. Construction of the line began in January, 1895, only to be brought to a halt by the 'Great Snow' when the Island suffered from being covered in many feet of snow which disrupted life for many days. When construction work recommenced in early February over 100 men were put to work, working upwards from a point near the Mines washing floor. In March the workforce was doubled but a strike, protesting at the 21 shilling wage for a 60 hour week, caused a small delay.

The Snaefell Power Station as it was when built in 1895. The flue from the boiler house passed under the track to the chimney on the other side.

The boilers provided steam for five Mather and Platt engines each coupled to a 60 Kw Hopkinson dynamo. Steam generation finished in 1924 and was replaced by a rotary converter supplied from the Laxey Power Station. The ruins of today are the site of the present substation.

The scene in Laxey on the opening day of the Snaefell Mountain Railway, 21st August, 1895. To the left, in cloak, is Dr Edward Hopkinson, Engineer. Beside him, in bowler hat, is Mr Alexander Bruce.

The revised Snaefell line terminus of 1897 before being moved to its present site in 1898. Behind Snaefell Car 2 is Dumbell's Row, cottages for the miners while to the right can be seen the 'deads' from the Great Laxey Mine.

It was not known at the time of construction whether electric tramcars could climb the 1 in 12 gradient by wheel adhesion alone and so it was decided to adopt the Fell Incline Railway system. This consisted of a double-headed centre rail between the running rails and which was gripped by additional horizontal driving wheels. The gripping system had been invented by John Barraclough Fell who was the father of George Fell, the latter having carried out a survey on behalf of the Douglas to Snaefell railway project in 1887. However, it had been proved elsewhere as construction continued that electric traction was possible on such gradients by normal wheel adhesion alone and so the Fell Gear was dispensed with, although the centre rail was retained for braking purposes.

In order to assist in the construction work, the powerful steam locomotive 'Caledonia' was hired from the Manx Northern Railway for a weekly rent of £20. A gauge of 3 feet 6 inches was chosen for the Snaefell line, the extra six inch of gauge being required to accommodate the proposed Fell Gear. It was therefore necessary to lay a temporary third rail to 3 feet gauge to allow 'Caledonia' to operate.

By May of 1895 a second gang was put to work at the summit, working downwards towards the other gang who were by now cutting a shelf into the rock face for the line at Lhergy Veg, well above Laxey. A power station to generate the line's electricity was constructed at a point just below the mountain road, which was roughly the halfway point of the line, its siting being dictated by the limitations in the transmission of the Direct Current through the overhead wires. Messrs Mather and Platt were again appointed as electrical contractors and installed in the power station four boilers supplying steam to five 120 hp engines each coupled to a 60 Kw dynamo. The entire equipment was lowered down the mountainside from the mountain road by block and tackle. Mr Willis of Mather and Platt slept on the site for 14 days during the installation period and was responsible for erecting nearly ten miles of overhead wire from the centre poles, this being accomplished in eight days. The power station was the most powerful on the Island at the time and was dominated by a 60 feet high chimney.

Such was the speed of construction that the line, just over 4½ miles, was ready for official inspection by Messrs Rich and Cardew on 16th August and, approval given, the line was opened for public service on 21st August. During the rest of the season 900 passengers were carried each day.

The passenger stock consisted of six tramcars which were built by G F Milnes of Birkenhead and similar to cars 10 - 13 which had joined the coastal railway. The Snaefell cars seat 48 passengers and when built were only glazed in the driving cabs at each end, but by 1896 had sliding windows fitted and clerestory roofs added the following year. The electrical equipment was again supplied by Mather and Platt. Each bogie was equipped with two 25 hp motors giving a total of 100 hp which made these cars the most powerful in Britain at that time. The Fell rail brakes were fitted at the outer end of each bogie and consisted of a caliper brake fitted with soft iron shoes which acted against the side of the Fell Rail. In practice, the brake shoes needeed replacing after an average of six descents from the summit. At the opposite, inner end, of each bogie is mounted a pair of horizontal guide wheels which act upon the centre rail and serve to prevent derailments. As on the coastal tramway, each car was provided with a pair of roof-mounted bow collectors to collect the current from the overhead wires. When the coastal tramcars were altered to operate with trolley poles in 1898, the Snaefell cars retained their bow collectors in order to prevent dewiring in high winds. The overhead wire is supported at the centre poles at a height higher than the bow collectors so that when passing the pole, the collector momentarily loses contact with the wire. However, current collection is maintained by the other collector which is still in contact with the wire between the poles.

In addition to the passenger cars, there were several other items of rolling stock. No 7, or 'Maria' as it was christened, was a six ton open wagon underframe with twin cabs used for freight. Each winter it was equipped with bogies and electrical equipment from a passenger car, usually No 5, and carried the next season's stock of coal to the power station. (It was last used during construction of a radar station at the summit for the Air Ministry in the mid-1950s and the remains can still be seen next to the car shed). A four-wheeled wagon was built by Hurst Nelson in 1895 to convey goods to the summit hotel, and remained in use until 1982 when it succumbed. There is also a four-wheeled tower wagon used to maintain the overhead wires.

In order to house the six trams, a brick depot was constructed at the lower terminus near Dumbell's Row and is still in use today. The regular day-to-day maintenance is carried out here but the major winter overhauls are carried out at the Derby Castle depot. As the two systems are of different gauge, a dual gauge siding was laid in Laxey station in 1931 to enable the cars to be transferred to 3 feet gauge trucks for the journey to Douglas. A new workshop is currently being erected at the depot which will enable all overhauls to be carried out there in future.

The original terminus of the line was situated next to the car depot and passengers from the Coast Tramway faced a lengthy walk through Laxey Village and ascent of a stone stepway to the Snaefell terminus. This was alleviated in part in 1897 when the Snaefell line was extended to a new terminus at the bottom of Mine's Road. In 1898 the Snaefell line was further extended to the present terminus at the new joint station.

Following the opening of the Snaefell line, the entire system was sold by the Snaefell Association to become part of the Isle of Man Tramways and Electric Power Company undertaking, for a sum of £72,500. It later transpired that the actual cost of construction was less than £40,000.

(Below) The 1895 Summit Hotel was a low wooden structure replaced in 1905 by this imposing building which stood until 1982 when it was gutted by a fire. It was rebuilt in 1984.

THE EXTENSION TO RAMSEY

The results being obtained by Isle of Man Tramways and Electric Power, with two electric lines, the horse trams and Douglas cable cars, were indeed encouraging. The total number of passengers carried in 1895 on the horse trams and electric lines (excluding Snaefell) approached 2 million. The forty minute Laxey journey attracted 10,477 in one day. 2,500 tons of goods had also been carried during the year. To pay for the Snaefell Tramway, capital had been increased to £315,000 and half yearly dividends of 6% on preference shares and 8½% on ordinary shares for the second half of the year were paid. Similar dividends were repeated in 1896 when profits rose to £17,822 despite bad weather and struggles with the Douglas cable line. The electric lines had carried 591,667 passengers out of a total of 2,399,559 on all four lines. Two new car sheds were added to Derby Castle to accommodate the four new cars of 1895 and the fifteen trailers of the fleet. The rustic ticket office, still a feature of Derby Castle terminus was built in 1897.

A confident Mr Bruce was now intent on undertaking the extension of the Douglas and Laxey Tramway to Ramsey. A bill had already been introduced to Tynwald in April 1896 by a London based company which was keen to get in on the act. This was counter-petitioned in October of that year by IOMT & EP Co to build a line of their own and the other group withdrew. In a new petition, presented in March 1897, the line was shown extending from the revised Laxey terminus of 1896 (a little closer to the centre of the village) across the Glen Roy river and over the cross roads, on the main road near the present Laxey station, to the 1897 Snaefell line terminus. A new scheme was proposed a month later, whereby the line travelled through a tunnel to emerge at the Snaefell terminus. The Douglas and Laxey Tramway (Extension to Ramsey) Act was passed by Tynwald in May 1897. The new line was legally a separate undertaking, with its own financial set up and to which I O M T & E P Co were allowed to contract for the construction work.

Preliminary construction work began in August though, officially, this was not until 1st November. Two separate construction gangs were put to work that winter. One worked south from Ballure and the Manx Northern Railway, anxious to earn some revenue, hired their engine No 1 'Ramsey' to assist at £2 10s per day, being dragged through the streets of Ramsey on timbers and short sections of rail to Ballure. The second gang worked northwards from Laxey

The picturesque Laxey Station was built in 1898 ready to receive the lines from Derby Castle and the extension to Ramsey. At the same time the Snaefell line was brought into the station. The large refreshment room in the centre was destroyed by fire in 1917. On the right is today's booking office, formerly that of the Snaefell line.

and had the assistance of I O M Railway's engine No 2 *Derby*. The company also purchased an engine of its own, an 0-4-0 saddle tank engine built by Andrew Barclay in 1892, and 45 ballast wagons. (In 1900 this engine was sold to Douglas Corporation to work on the construction of their West Baldwin Reservoir). In addition, 30 horses were borrowed from the Douglas tramway.

At Laxey, there was another change of plan, the subway proposal being dropped. Instead, a new station was planned on land owned by the Great Laxey Mining Company, this being the garden of the Mines Captain's house and adjacent to Christ Church. To bring the Douglas-Laxey line in to the new station a handsome, curved four-arched viaduct across Glen Roy was begun in March, 1898, and completed by its contractors, Mark Carine, in only four months. The Snaefell line was extended from its 1897 terminus into the new station and its terminus building re-erected on the new site. A large wooden restaurant was constructed (destroyed by fire in 1917) and lawns laid, with rustic seats and kiosks.

At Bulgham Bay, some 2½ miles north of Laxey, the line's summit of 588 feet above sea level is reached at a point where the line runs along the cliff face, with, in places, almost a sheer drop to the sea below. The construction work here was by far the biggest and most spectacular engineering feat of the entire railway. Work began on 15th November 1897. The main Laxey to Ramsey road already ran round the cliff face and the Highway Board allowed the road to be closed for three months. The rock face had to be cut away and the roadway moved inland some 30 feet so that the new tramway could occupy the roadway's former position, being supported by the old road's dry stone wall. In one place, however, the line was built on a partly cantilevered shelf. The road was reopened the following April, but was not completed to the Highway Board's satisfaction until April 1901! The road was again closed in January 1903, this time for six months, to allow the tracks to be moved further inland onto solid rock, the cliff being cut back to allow the road to be moved in by a similar distance. The part cantilevered track was removed. Final completion came in October 1904.

At the mid-point of the line, at Ballagorry, a deep cutting was required and single line only was laid through the cutting. A short distance further north was Ballaglass Glen, where a new generating station was positioned. The line at this point runs on an embankment above the fast flowing Corony river, next to which the new station was built. The electrical constructors were Dick, Kerr and Co. Two Robb Armstrong tandem compound engines, rated at 180 hp at

The ornate Ballaglass Power Station housed two of the new 1904 six-pole 150Kw converters built by Kolben of Prague. The Power Station also contained the two Robb Armstrong steam engines of 1898 which were coupled to generators supplied by the Electric Construction Company of Wolverhampton, these continuing in use until 1934.

175 rpm, were each coupled to an ECC six-pole multipolar generator. Each generator produced 240 amps at 500 volts. A second room contained a Chloride battery of 260 cells rated to give 140 amps for six hours, charged by a 500v/150v shunt wound motor generator. It was also possible to charge the battery at Ballaglass from the turbine house at Laxey (built in 1899), via the underground feeder system. An additional feeder also ran 2½ miles northwards from Ballaglass to assist in maintaining voltage on the steeper gradients which were kept to 1 in 24 as a maximum.

On the southern coastal outskirts of Ramsey it was proposed to construct a sweeping promenade to the Ramsey Pier. The new promenade was to be 50 feet wide to accommodate the railway, road and footpath. However, the scheme was abandoned and the railway's approach to Ramsey kept at a higher level on the cliff tops, descending across Ballure Glen and behind the houses on Waterloo Road to a town centre terminus. By May, 1898, work was so far advanced that preparations were made for opening the extension for the summer traffic. The line had been engineered on a grand scale and over 1,000 men had been employed, wages being 4d an hour despite a threat to strike for a 4½d rate. A total of 250,000 tons of spoil had been removed and 60,000 tons of ballast laid.

The overhead of the Laxey - Ramsey line was constructed for the use of the now familiar overhead trolley system. At the same time the Douglas - Laxey section was similarly altered. Each car was fitted with a Boston Pivotal trolley base and trolley poles with fixed heads, the bow collectors being removed. To work the Ramsey line, nine open cross-bench cars were ordered from G. F. Milnes. Only five (Nos. 14 to 18) were, in the event, motored whilst the remaining four (Nos. 19 - 22) were used as trailers, becoming Nos. 40 - 43 in 1899. They were eventually motored in 1903 becoming Nos. 24 - 27.

By July, 1898, the line was completed as far as Ballure and was subsequently inspected by Colonel Rich and Major Cardew on 18th July. Rich did not approve of a number of points, such as the lack of protection of the single line at Ballagorry. These points were attended to and the line to Ballure was officially opened on Tuesday, 2nd August, by His Excellency The Lieutenant Governor Lord Henniker who with the Board of Management and various other Island dignitaries travelled from Douglas on two of the new open

The Ballure Bridge was built in 1899 to complete the route to Ramsey. Here a tram, clearly marked 'DOUGLAS, LAXEY AND RAMSEY ELECTRIC RAILWAY' is setting out on the 17 miles to Douglas. Taken from a glass negative plate, the photograph dates from the early 1900s and was taken by Cowen's Studio, Ramsey.

cross-bench cars, suitably bedecked with flags. An opening speech was made by His Excellency at Ballure, followed by a reception in the Queen's Hotel, Ramsey.

The Ramsey line closed on 24th October, after the 1898 season, to allow further work to be carried out and the extension of the line into Ramsey itself. It was at first planned to terminate the line at the Pavilion beyond Walpole Drive, but the Company had purchased the Palace Concert Hall (later to become the Plaza Cinema) with the intention of making its grounds the terminus. The plan was nearly scrapped with Bruce refusing to pay for a toll on the line which the town commissioners were insisting upon. However, their demands were dropped and the line through to the Palace was constructed, thus occupying the present site, 17.75 miles (28.6Km) from Derby Castle.

A bridge across Ballure Glen was constructed by Francis Morton and Co. of Garston, Liverpool and, unlike the viaduct at Laxey (and Minorca), was constructed with four iron girders, arranged in pairs, each pair spanning a gap of 80 feet, with a girder under each rail. At Walpole Drive, the lines were laid in grooved rail with the overhead poles erected at the side of the line. Here, the line was officially classed as a street tramway, although the surfacing of the tramway section was never carried out. The line was reopened to Ballure on 17th June, whilst the opening of the final section to Ramsey took place on 24th July 1899. A half hourly service was operated and the return fare to Douglas was 3s 6d or 2s 6d after 4 pm.

Four new cars, the 'winter saloons,' were delivered from G F Milnes and Co. and became Nos. 19 - 22. These beautifully finished cars have been the backbone of the timetabled services ever since. Five new open cross-bench trailers, Nos. 44-48, were also delivered from the same builder. Finishing touches were being applied, such as the ornamental shrubs along the Douglas - Laxey section. Further waiting rooms were built at Half Way House, Garwick, Ballabeg and South Cape, most of which still exist. Apart from transport and electricity supply, the company sought to expand in other ways. They had an interest in many of the glens the tramway passed which were a tourist attraction in themselves. Licensed hotels and refreshment rooms were built at Laxey, Douglas, the Bungalow, Snaefell Summit and Dhoon Glen; there was even talk of the company setting up its own brewery! In contrast a granite quarry was developed to supply local needs and also for export through Ramsey. Horse and carts were needed but, to smooth the transfer of the granite, three Bonner wagons from Toledo, Ohio, were received in September, 1899; these could be transferred from road to a railway underframe by means of ramps. Also, in 1899, the water of the Laxey river, much used by the Mines Washing Floors, was harnessed to drive turbines housed below the Laxey Power Station. The turbine power plant was designed by Joshua Shaw and was intended to augment the power supply and close down the steam stations in winter. The peak summer load on all three power stations had now reached 2,200 hp, all produced by coal imported from South Wales. On 17th December 1899 Alexander Bruce started the Laxey turbines. It was to be his last public duty as he was soon to be overcome by illness.

A view of the early Ramsey station adjoining the Palace Theatre which was converted into the Plaza Cinema in 1934 and now demolished. A waiting room was built along the side of the theatre and the original booking office can be seen on the right.

THE MANX ELECTRIC RAILWAY COMPANY

The construction of the electric tramway system had attracted world-wide interest but it was soon to attract publicity of a different kind. The electrical engineering, much of it of an experimental nature, had been a costly affair. The cost of the Laxey - Ramsey extension amounted to £153,412 with land claims of £24,000 outstanding. This had been by far the company's most expensive project which was to bring the total expenditure by the I O M T & E P Co to £518,000, of which only £366,000 had been raised. Bruce had been borrowing heavily and, to keep up appearances, had been maintaining dividends out of capital rather than earnings. As early as January 1899 the company secretary had resigned fearing the worst, while the auditors contrived to show a favourable balance sheet. The company owed £150,000 to Dumbell's Bank which had been arranged by Bruce and underwritten by Parr's Bank in England. In February 1900 the English bank foreclosed on the loan, an event which was to lead to the collapse of Dumbell's Bank with disastrous results on the Island; it was a catastrophe to the I O M T & E P Co. Bruce, the guiding light, was largely held to blame. Warrants for his arrest, together with bank officials and the tramways auditors, were issued, though in the case of Bruce the warrant was withdrawn as he had had a relapse and it was felt his arrest would have proved fatal. As it happened, he died in September 1900 and the one time hero in finacial and political circles departed unmourned.

That summer of 1900 saw crisis meetings of directors and shareholders. There were those who hoped to raise fresh capital but, in the end, liquidation was imposed, the death knell of The Isle of Man Tramways and Electric Power Company. The tramways were allowed to continue operations under the company engineer and secretary, Mr Joshua Shaw. Contingency plans saw the Dhoon quarry closed with the loss of a hundred jobs and the hotels were rented out. The order for the sale was not made until July 1901 by which time an invaluable inventory of all the company's assets had been prepared by Mr Ramsey B. Moore, later Attorney General, on behalf of the liquidator, Mr William H. Walker.

A major engineering feat was the construction of the track nearly 600 feet above Bulgham Bay. Unhappy with the original construction, the newly formed M E R Company decided to move the line inland onto a more secure rock base. The work was carried out from January to May 1903 under the supervision of resident engineer Mr Frank Edmundson.

When tenders were opened on 7th September 1901, Mr Walker turned down an offer from the British Electric Traction Company for £225,000 for all five lines (horse, cable and the three electric) as being insufficient. A final offer by Douglas Corporation of £50,000 for the profitable horse trams and the loss-making cable cars was accepted. It was not until January 1902 that another bid for the electric lines was received, this time for £250,000 from a Continental merchant banker acting for 'a Manchester syndicate.' The offer was accepted but it was not until September that a final settlement was made. On the 1st November 1902, THE MANX ELECTRIC RAILWAY COMPANY was incorporated with its registered office in London. Of all the shareholders, the Greenwell family of stockbrokers were by far the most prominent and they came to look upon the enterprise as a family affair. The authorised capital was £500,000 half of which was in debenture stock and the other half split equally between preferential and ordinary shares. The new company purchased the entire railway from the Manchester syndicate on 30th November for £370,000.

During this period Mr Joshua Shaw left to become engineer to the Mersey Electric Railway and Mr Frank Edmundson took over as engineer. A young Manxman, Harold Brown, moved from the Steam Packet Company to become Manager, the first appointment by the new board. The interim period had seen the visit of the newly-crowned King Edward V11 and Queen Alexandra on 2nd August 1902. After touring parts of the Island by carriage they returned from Douglas to the royal yacht at Ramsey by the electric railway. For this royal occasion, saloon trailer No 59, draped in purple, was coupled to one of the series 19-22 motor cars.

Of immediate concern to the new company was the permanent way between Douglas and Laxey where reballasting and replacement of sleepers had stopped during the liquidation. At the request of superintendent Robert Newell, 120 tons of rail, 20,000 tons of ballast and 5,200 sleepers were provided. Drains on either side of the track were cleared and fencing repaired. Not happy with the

In 1903 the M E R Company replaced the discredited DC supply with AC supply, installing at Laxey two generators of Belgian design each capable of producing 7,000 volts. Laxey Power Station in the Glen Road became the centre for the new AC supply system.

partially cantilevered track at Bulgham, the new company decided to move the track inland on to solid rock. Spoil removed from Bulgham amounted to 46,735 tons by the end of 1903.

Even though much of the electrical equipment was less than ten years old, such were the advances being made that it was already considered obsolescent. Determined to upgrade the equipment, the company employed consultants to advise. The DC system of generating was now discredited and AC generators and distribution was recommended. This work was undertaken by Witting Eborall and Co. The Douglas generator plant was taken out of service and Laxey became the main centre of the new AC system with support from Ballaglass. New Bellis and Morcom triple expansion engines of 400 hp now provided the power to drive high tension AC generators producing current of 7,000 volts. This supply was taken through new AC feeders to rotary converter sub-staions at Douglas, Groudle, Ballaglass and Snaefell, as well as the Laxey Power Station. Coal was supplied through Laxey harbour and the Power Station operated from 6.30 am to midnight during the summer season, and only occasionally during the winter in support of the turbines. Ballaglass operated only during the summer. Steam working at Snaefell continued until 1924 when a second rotary converter was transferred from Laxey. The cars were re-equipped by Witting Eborall and Co. with improved motors and control equipment; the increased efficiency gained meant that the Douglas-Laxey run was reduced from 40 to 30 minutes.

The 'M E R,' as it became affectionately known, also repurchased the Dhoon quarry and built a car and goods shed at Laxey, and a goods shed at Ramsey. New trailer cars were added to the fleet and shelters provided at stops where non existed. While heavily dependent on the summer traffic, the management made every effort to increase freight handling. A new goods shed was built at Douglas on the site of the old boiler house and new goods vehicles were ordered until a total of 29 were available by 1912. The Dhoon quarry was providing granite paving setts and low-grade road material, both in big demand. Agricultural goods and livestock were catered for, with regular milk collections. Luggage to and from Douglas meant busy weekend handlings during the summer. In addition to the goods and parcel service for locals the line played an important part in carrying bulk mail for the Post Office, and by May 1904, a mail collection by conductors from lineside boxes was introduced, providing more revenue. A generator remained in use at Derby Castle for the supply to customers in Onchan and Douglas, the town not having its own supply until 1922.

With the mountain road closed at the Bungalow for the Gordon Bennett Car Trials on 14th September 1905, single line working was in operation, three cars on each line. On the return at Lhergy Veg the lead car stopped for some unknown reason resulting in the middle car (No 6) being badly damaged front and rear as a result of a collision involving the three cars. The Company had to pay considerable compensation to the injured passengers. This is the only serious accident which has occurred on the Snaefell line.

As part of a carnival event in 1911 the M E R arranged to light the promenade which so impressed the Corporation that they took immediate steps to provide permanent decorative lighting, thus being able to boast of being the first resort to have illuminations.

A total of 535,021 passengers was carried in 1906, earning profits of £34,279 for the company. This was encouraging and prudent management put the undertaking on a secure footing. New cars and trailers arrived in 1906 and the Snaefell Summit Hotel was opened in the same year. The scenic beauty of the line and the Manx glens were the main attractions and these were not neglected. In 1906 the company bought the Laxey Glen and Gardens, already magnificently laid out, and popular military bands became a feature of the entertainment throughout the season. At Groudle a share of the glen admission receipts continued to be paid to the company while a toll house at the corner beyond the Glen entrance charged for the use of the road along the side of the track as far as the Half Way House, a practice which continued into the 1920s. Ballaglass Glen was at first rented and then purchased by the M.E.R., admission charges being collected at the entrance kiosk. Garwick Glen was developed along similar lines to Groudle by the owner who paid 1d. per adult admitted to the company. Dhoon Glen was rented by the M E R who paid 1.75d per admission to the owners.

The new company regained control of all its licensed hotels and a manager was appointed to supervise the six hotels and refreshment rooms. The M E R hotels were the Strathallan (at Derby Castle and now the Terminus Tavern), Laxey Station, Bungalow, Snaefell, Tholt y Will (Sulby Glen) and Dhoon, the latter being an imposing building but burnt down in 1932 and never rebuilt. As a final touch the M E R brought the first motor charabancs to the Island in 1907 to connect the Bungalow with Tholt y Will where a large refreshment room was built at the head of the Glen. Trips to these parts were advertised as to the 'Heart of the Manx Switzerland.'

The two Argus vehicles were registered MN 67 and MN 68 and were joined in 1913 by a De Dion numbered MN 479. After the First World War, the charabancs were changed to 30-seat Caledons - MN 1053 and MN 1054. These continued in use until 1926 when three Model 'T' Ford vehicles took over until 1937 when they were replaced by Bedford 20-seat WLBs registered MN 8685 and MN 8686.

Thus, by 1907, the new company had laid the foundations of the operations of the Manx Electric Railway which were to endure for half a century as a private enterprise, playing a significant part in the Island's tourist industry and providing millions of visitors with the pleasure of enjoying this attractive and charming part of the Island. The company was rewarded by a steady climb in passenger totals until, in 1913, a total of over 700,000 was exceeded for the first time. Although ordinary share holders had received only two dividends (2% for 1913) debenture and preferential share holders gained a good return. It had also been possible to build up a reserve fund which was to help the M E R tide over the lean years of the First World War.

In 1907 the M E R introduced the first charabancs to the Island for the purpose of conveying passengers to and from the top of Tholt y Will and Sulby Glen with its large rustic tea-room. Seen at the Bungalow Hotel, built in 1896, are MN 67 and 68 on the right, both Argus vehicles, which were joined by a De Dion, MN 479, in 1913.

1919-1939 THE INTER-WAR YEARS

Unlike the Isle of Man Steam Railway, the war years found little work for the Manx Electric Railway. The Snaefell line was closed and passengers carried dropped to 109,000 in 1916 with the financial deficits rising each year to £31,000. The Laxey rustic refreshment room was destroyed by fire in 1917 and never rebuilt. A wage settlement, as a result of the Island 'bread' strike, secured a wage settlement with the management of 6d. an hour for a 56 hour week. Previous wages had been 30 shillings a week for unlimited hours in summer and 24s.6d. in winter. It was, therefore, with relief that the tourist season of 1919 saw the holiday-makers return in their thousands and the year produced sufficient revenue to erase the wartime deficiencies.. The following year was again satisfactory but 1921 saw passengers fall to 667,000 thus halving profits. However, it had been possible to carry out improvements to the power supply which had been planned for 1914. A turbo-alternator and transformer were installed at Laxey and new Stirling boilers replaced the Climax ones and were installed in a new boiler house on the site which had been originally occupied by the three Galloway boilers of 1894-8. Well-known personality Bertram Kelly, chief assistant to Mr Edmundson, left the company in 1922 to take charge of the construction of Douglas Corporation's first electric power station at North Quay and in the following year he became the first borough electrical engineer.

The all-important passenger figures began to fluctuate from season to season, often reflecting economic conditions on the 'mainland.' The year 1922 saw the best total yet achieved - 727,000 - which was bettered in 1925 when over 789,000 passengers were recorded. The meticulous company records show that 333,755 passenger miles and 43,054 goods miles had been covered that year. It is interesting to note that 1925 had also been the best year for the I O M Steam Railway with a record 1,344,620 passengers carried. For both railways it was a significant year because a gradual decline began, beginning in 1926 with the General Strike followed by the recessionary years of the early 1930s. Figures for the M E R fell below the critical 500,000 mark though company finances remained sound as a result of careful management and maintenance of resources. Matters were not helped by the arrival of the first 'bus services on the Island.

The excellent safety record of the railway was marred by an incident on 8th August 1928 when Car No 1 and trailer 39, full of passengers, were running down hill from Ballabeg until being brought to a stop at Fairy Cottage to pick up two permanent way staff returning to Laxey. While a ladder was being affixed to the car, Car No 16 with trailer 56, similarly loaded, appeared round the bend at normal speed but the motorman was unable to bring his car to a stop, causing a collision in which all vehicles, excepting the leading car, were badly damaged. More serious were the injuries sustained by 32 of the passengers some of whom, like the motorman, jumped before the impact. Many received leg injuries and fractures. At the official enquiry Mr Edmundson stated that over 60 million passengers had been carried on the line without mishap. As a precaution, marker boards were placed at the entrance and exit points of blind curves, indicating that stopping between the boards was no longer permitted.

The M E R was to suffer a series of disasters beginning in April 1930 with a fire at Laxey Car Depot. It was late Saturday night, with the depot unmanned, when the fire was discovered and Laxey Fire Brigade summoned. The nearby hydrant was found to be covered with tarmacadam, rendering it useless. Douglas Fire Brigade was called and water was pumped from the Glen Roy river but the fire, with flames leaping through the roof, had taken hold and the buiding was engulfed when the doors were opened to rescue some of the vehicles. Cars Nos. 3, 4, 8 and 24, together with seven trailers, 34, 35, 38, 39, 40, 41, and 44, were completely destroyed. Also three tower wagons, a mail van and quantities of tools and equipment were consumed by the fire, thought to have been caused by a smouldering cigarette igniting dust on one of the vehicles. The two trailers, 50 and 60, that were pulled clear were badly burnt but were later returned to service. Those still in the depot were scrapped and used for spares . Insurance enabled the depot to be rebuilt and three new trailer cars to be purchased from English Electric.

During September at the end of the 1930 season, torrential rain affected all parts of the Island and flood waters poured down the slopes of Snaefell. Thousands of tons of debris were carried by the Laxey river only to become dammed behind the weir of the old hydro-electric plant, diverting the flood water which washed away the adjoining road and flooded nearby houses. The Power Station was submerged causing damage to much of the plant which had to be stripped, dried and cleaned. Water power was restored after a week but it took a further six weeks to bring all the equipment back into operation. During most of this time the village was without its electricity supply and a Relief Fund

DERBY

was set up to help householders who had lost many of their possessions. One of the longest legal cases in Manx history resulted in the company being held responsible for the damage to the road because of the blocked weir and they had to remove 4,000 to 5,000 tons of debris. They also had to pay legal costs and the unhappy episode cost the M E R nearly £3,500. In charge of the flood repairs was Mr J F Watson. He had been an apprentice with the company and returned in 1929. In 1936 he became Chief Assistant Engineer to Mr Edward Barnes who was appointed company Manager and Engineer following the death of Mr Edmundson. Another blow to the company was the complete destruction by fire of the imposing building of the Dhoon Hotel in 1932.

Winter work during this period involved the increasing use of the railway by school children, especially following the opening of the Ramsey Grammar School. There was also a big demand for granite chippings during 1933-34 from the Dhoon Quarry when the King Edward Road was resurfaced, as was the mountain section of the T T Course. More work came from the extension of the north promenade in Douglas during 1935, one of the winter work schemes. Public supply of electricity served many parts of Onchan, Baldrine and Laxey. But by 1929 the Pulrose Power Station was in operation for Douglas Corporation and the Isle of Man Electricity Board had been formed to provide electricity for other parts of the Island. Their first power station was built at Peel. It has been said that had the directors of the M E R been resident on the Island they might well have foreseen the public demand for electricity and, with the company's expertise, extended this side of their business, thus providing a steady income to support the more tenuous railway operation.

With the passing of the years, much of the 'new' generator equipment was now over twenty years old; generating costs were amounting to £5,000 a year. Rather than invest in new plant the M E R company reached an agreement with the Electricity Board in 1934 to supply all their needs. This ensured an initial cheap supply at the beginning of each season but as the summer peak approached a 'maximum demand' charge was applied and continued for the rest of the year. The company had to bear the cost, on a hire-purchase basis, of all new equipment and transmission lines involved. The new layout consisted of six rectifier substations to convert the AC supply to DC for the cars. These substations are at Douglas, Groudle, Laxey, Snaefell, Ballaglass and Bellevue. Of these, Laxey, Ballaglass and Bellevue are fed directly from the public supply at 33,000 volts while Douglas, Groudle and Snaefell are fed at 6,600 volts AC through the 1904 lines from a purpose-built transformer at Laxey. To reinforce the 550v DC feeders an additional overhead line was added from Douglas to Groudle, supplying the 1904 feeders, and beyond Groudle it is carried on pole-mounted brackets all the way to Ramsey. Steam generation at Ballaglass stopped in 1934. The water turbine at Laxey continued in use until the new system was completed in readiness for May 1935. The new Laxey substation is positioned near the revised tram station of 1895-6, before the building of the Rencell bridge. Increased motor traffic on Manx roads saw trolley-activated traffic lights installed at Half Way House in 1934 and at Ballabeg and Ballure in 1936. The lights are now treadle-operated.

The second half of the decade was something of a 'purple patch' with passenger figures rising from 543,000 in 1935 to 570,000 in 1937, allowing part of the debt to the Electricity Board to be paid off. The directors, under Sir Bernard Greenwell, met in the boardroom at Strathallan every three months and were content to leave the specialised running of operations to their company officials. However, it was imperative that each Monday morning a full report of the previous week's activities, with detailed figures, was despatched to company secretary, Mr S A Young, at 10-11 Finsbury Circus, London. Copies of these reports occupied considerable space at No 1 Strathallan Crescent, the railway's local headquarters. Employees recall that it was a good firm to work for, having a reputation for high standards in all matters and a discipline that had to be obeyed, including no smoking on the premises or cars.

(Opposite) A typical busy summer scene at Derby Castle in the 1920s and '30s with trams kept busy coping with the awaiting queues of passengers. On the left, horse trams are arriving at the ornate shelter built in 1896 close to which is the rustic 1897 booking office of the M E R, still in use today. The terminus took its name from the former private residence of Derby Castle whose grounds were taken over for the development of an entertainments complex including the Pavilion Dance Hall and Theatre, performances in the latter being punctuated by the rumble of passing trams. Behind the theatre is the entrance to the Derby Castle Tram Depot. The Derby Castle buildings were demolished in the late 1960s to make way for Summerland. The photograph also shows the north promenade before being widened in 1935. (Keig Collection)

The daily routine of the busy summer days started with a thorough inspection of the track and overhead wires, a member of the permanent way staff walking a section so that the whole line from Douglas to Ramsey was covered. First cars through were the early morning service cars but by 10 am all 24 cars with trailers were in place for the day's work. Much of the service was played by ear and in response to telephone calls. 'Specials' were the order of the day right through to closing the line late at night. Douglas saw cars leaving every three minutes for Onchan Head (White City), Howstrake Holiday Camp and Groudle, with its many attractions including illuminations, concerts and dancing, while a miniature railway took passengers to a creek where polar bears and sea lions were popular. Despite a basic 48 hour week, long hours were worked by a staff of over a hundred, with no thought of taking a break during the summer season. There were permanent salaried stationmasters and assistants at Douglas, Laxey and Ramsey while Groudle, Garwick (for Garwick Glen), Bungalow and Summit had stationmasters on duty for the summer. There were booking clerks at Douglas (2), Laxey and Summit, with kiosk attendants at White City, Sulby Glen, Dhoon and Ballaglass. Five inspectors were employed to supervise the operations. Catering staff were also required for the hotels and refreshment rooms. Many of the Derby Castle Depot staff came out for the summer as platform staff (a tradition which still continues today) leaving a skeleton maintenance staff under the depot foreman who issued instructions and detailed crews to selected cars. Left behind were joiners, painters, cleaners, a blacksmith, an armature winder and several general labourers and apprentices. Each of the six sub-stations were continually manned. At Groudle the traction battery continued in use to help reduce the maximum tariff of the Electricity Board. To even consumption an ingenious system was devised whereby cars were despatched from Douglas according to the passing of

This small toll-house was built in 1895 at Groudle to collect tolls for use of the private road to Balldromma Beg, a practice which continued into the 1920s. Behind was positioned the Groudle Battery House, which was used until 1944, and the present sub-station.

Garwick station once boasted a stationmaster in summer to cope with the busy traffic resulting from the attractions of Garwick Glen and beach. Here passengers are waiting for the return to Douglas.

Queues of passengers at Laxey waiting for a tram to Snaefell Summit. It is obviously a fine day with the hope of good views from the top.

The M E R made full use of the attractions of the various glens along the coastal route. Ballaglass Halt also had a kiosk where admission tickets and refreshments were sold.

marker counters on an electrically-driven belt representing the line to Laxey, the idea being to avoid too many starts on uphill sections at the same time.

Retired railway employee Artie Walmsley recalls those years which, for him, began in 1936 as a conductor. Having set up home in Ramsey he was glad to find a job and, with the help of his wife set about memorising all the different fares. The one shilling single to Douglas was no problem but the many intermediate fares with pennies and halfpennies took some learning. Dressed in his navy blue suit, white shirt, tie and black shoes he reported to Ramsey station at 6.30 am for the 6.45 mail and boat car arriving in Douglas at 8.00 am. There were twenty such scheduled services during weekdays to which were added numerous specials. Artie recalls trying to avoid the evening Groudle specials as they seemed to go on for ever with a queue stretching 200 yards round the corner below the hotel. Nevertheless, Artie revelled in the 'atmosphere' of the railway with the summer revellers and, looking back, he 'loved every minute of it.' At the end of the day he reported to Strathallan Crescent with his ticket receipts to be checked. If not on the last service car from Douglas at 11.00 pm , arriving Ramsey at 12.10 midnight, he would return on the staff car which dropped off employees as they went home for the night. Awaiting Artie would be his only cooked meal of the day, having to had make do on sandwiches and pies. Then it was off to bed for an early start next morning. Wages at that time were 11 pence farthing an hour and Artie worked all the hours he could during the week to bring home a decent wage. His wage packets show that £3.17.7 was an average before one shilling and eightpence had been deducted for health insurance, sick and hospital funds. The hours worked meant that he rarely saw his family during the summer though wet days he could be stood down for a few hours. One of the company perks, he recalls, was an occasional free pass which he could use on the cars! Winter time saw him employed on the track painting poles, trimming hedges, clearing ditches and laying new rails. As Easter approached he would join the gang preparing the Snaefell line in readiness for the season. He recalls with amusement painting the galvanised Bungalow hotel and using a sweeping brush to cover the roof with fresh green paint!

Saturday arrival figures by the steamers were studied to anticipate demand for the week, as was the weather which determined cars required for Snaefell. Fine days would see queues forming early in the morning for the popular Snaefell and Sulby Glen tour which cost 4s 6d including lunch. Fleetwood boat trips brought in additional thousands which saw queues stretching as far as the bottom of Summerhill for the departure to Laxey and Snaefell. Despatching the people in time for the boat return was a headache for the Laxey stationmaster. Special 'rover' tickets kept the weekdays particularly busy while the weekends were comparatively quiet and brought some respite. But the happy days were to come to an end in August 1939 as once again the war clouds gathered over Europe. By March 1940 the M E R staff had fallen to thirty with many of the facilities, including the Snaefell line, closed for the duration.

Dhoon Glen, with its waterfall and beach is still a favourite glen to explore. It was once rented by the M E R Company who built the Dhoon Glens Hotel as an added attraction. The large wooden building with refreshment rooms was destroyed by fire in 1932 and never rebuilt.

THE POST-WAR YEARS AND NATIONALISATION

The Second World War saw the railway operate a skeleton service mainly for the benefit of residents although some additional work was found in conveying aliens, interned in the hotels of Douglas and Ramsey, to work on farms. Numbers fell to below 100,000 passengers in 1940. In contrast, the steam railway was called upon to maintain a busy schedule, including many specials, to transport thousands of service personnel to the various training establishments set up throughout the Island. War work for the M E R included hauling thousands of tons of the Laxey mine 'deads' for use in constructing runways at R.A.F. Jurby. The maximum demand tariff of the Electricity Board ceased to apply and the Groudle traction battery went out of service in 1944. Government support was available but not used, a small profit being made though little was spent on maintenance. With the end of the war in Europe the summer visitors began to return, over 200,000 passengers using the railway in 1945.

Then began the post war boom which brought incredible scenes of activity throughout the whole system with the remainder of the decade seeing over 750,000 passengers a year being handled on the coastal and mountain lines. Queues were the order of the day, not only of passengers but also of cars and trailers as they returned to Derby Castle for the evening. The T T Race days saw as many as 2,000 on the Snaefell line as fans made their way to the favourite vantage point at the Bungalow where the hotel did a roaring trade in supplying refreshments. These were hectic days with long hours worked, with the staff, on a 48 hour week, earning considerable overtime. Like many of the M E R employess, conductor Artie Walmsley returned from war service changing his uniform to that of assistant stationmaster at Ramsey. He was kept busy on ticket sales, looking after the mail despatches and supervising the luggage and goods being handled. After a while he was made an inspector but he asked to be relieved of this position as his many calls for "Tickets, please," too often met with derisory cries of "Oh no, not again!" A move to Douglas saw him in charge of the busy Derby Castle ticket office where he remained happily until retirement in 1980. While fares were kept low in those post war years (5 shillings for the Douglas - Snaefell return) profits were good enabling a good return for shareholders and the debt to the Electrcity Board to be finally wiped out. Money was also available for the winter repair and maintenance work.

It was 'all systems go' as the railway returned to normal routine after the Second World War. The fleet of 24 cars and trailers were kept busy through near record seasons with peak periods seeing three minute departures from Derby Castle to cope with the traffic to White City (above), Howstrake Holiday Camp and Groudle.

The heady years of 1946-49 were to prove a final fling for the M E R Company. Holiday habits were changing and tourist figures began to decline resulting in passengers falling to 500,000 in 1950. At the same time wage rises had to be absorbed and the price of materials for essential repairs to track and stock rose alarmingly. Government reports on local transport, vital to the tourist industry, were initiated and the cost of replacing the 24 cars and trailers was estimated to be £110,000. That was in 1949, while six years later the cost of replacing the vehicle stock had risen to £312,000 with another £292,000 needeed to replace the track which was showing signs of wear and gradually being overrun by grass and weeds. To the experts in heavy railway operations who were invited to submit their views, it seemed economic sense to close the Ramsey extension and concentrate resources on maintaining the Laxey and Snaefell lines. The fact that the Ramsey line was a scenic route and an amenity to the tourist industry, whether in decline or not, does not seem to have been considered by the experts.

In 1949 Mr John Rowe became company secretary following the transfer of the company's London office to No 1 Strathallan Crescent. Mr Rowe had joined the office staff at Douglas in 1929 and in 1952 he became Joint Manager with Mr J F ('Jack') Watson who had been assistant to Mr Barnes who died that year. They were confronted with many problems as the company's fortunes continued to decline with mounting losses. Properties were sold off, including Dhoon and Ballaglass Glens to the I O M Forestry Board. The later Dhoon quarry had already passed to the Highways Board. Winter Sunday services were abandoned in 1951-2 for the first time and approaches were made to Government to close the line for the winter of 1953-4 and to permit increased fares for the following summer. While the latter was approved, the company was held to its statutory duty of providing a winter service. For the people of Maughold the railway was still their main form of transport despite the encroachment of buses. There was also much appreciation of the 'civility and courtesy' of M E R staff. The debenture and shareholders had the power to realise their assets and close the company but they chose the opposite, thus providing an amenity which was a loss to themselves.

Maintenance work had to be kept to a minimum but vital repairs to the timbers of Ballure bridge were made in August 1955. During the repairs single line operation, with staff, was introduced between Lewaigue and Ramsey. Car 22 from Ramsey with driver Tommy Stephens and Artie Walmsley conductor had reached the section between Bellevue and Lewaigue when they were suddenly confronted by Car 14 coming in the opposite direction on the same line. The ratchet car from Laxey had Fred Shepherton as driver and medical student Cliff Cowley as conductor who had not been informed of the single line operation. The result was a nasty collision which resulted in four passengers being injured, though not seriously.

At the end of 1955 the M E R directors, after supporting another year of overall losses, notified the Government that they would have to cease operations after the 1956 season. They were prepared to sell the railways for £70,000. Tynwald responded by appointing a sub-committee led by Mr J B Bolton MHK to look into the matter. It was this committee that called upon three British Rail specialists, headed by Mr M R Varley, which produced a figure of £674,000 for the

By 1955, the days of The Manx Electric Railway Co. Ltd. were numbered, resources only allowing the minimum of maintenance, such as the re-timbering of the track on Ballure Bridge.

replacement of vehicle stock and renewal of the track. Another commission which had been looking into the visiting industry had recently recommended that the coastal railway and the Snaefell line should be retained as a tourist attraction, implying Government assistance. However, the sub-committee recommended to Tynwald that no assistance should be given and it was even suggested that a road to the summit of Snaefell would be a better proposition! Their report was not accepted and another sub-committee was set up to look into ways of continuing the railway at a reasonable cost.

An inspection of the railway was made by another team of experts, this time headed by Mr J W Fowler, chairman of the Light Railway Transport League who was joined by Mr C T Humpidge of Bradford City Transport and, once again, Mr Varley of British Rail. This time their report was much more favourable saying the cost of maintenance need not be prohibitive if spread over a period, and that the value of such an historic railway was incalculable. In August 1956 the Tynwald committee met the M E R directors who were now prepared to sell the railway for £50,000, just about the scrap value of the hardware. That December Tynwald debated the matter in full with Deemster Sir Percy Cowley arguing strongly the case for retention; 70% of tourists regarded the scenic route as part of their holiday, it was of importance to Ramsey and it provided employment for a number of Manx people. The arguments won the day convincingly and in April 1957 the Bill was formally signed by Tynwald. The railway would be purchased and a ten year programme of renewals and renovations initiated under the newly constituted Manx Electric Railway Board.

On 1st June 1957 the railway was officially handed over at a ceremony at Derby Castle followed by Car 32, suitably decorated, making a trip to Groudle with passengers including the Lieutenant Governor Sir Ambrose Flux Dundas, Deemster Cowley, Mr H C Kerruish MHK, Sir Ralph Stephenson MLC, the first chairman of the new Board, Mr L Bond of the Tourist Board and the Joint Managers of the MER Company who continued in their positions. The other Tynwald Board members were Mr R C Stephens MHK and Mr A H Simcocks MHK. With power to co-opt they were joined by T W Billington, accountant, and Mr T W Kneale, a retired official of the North Western Railway of India, an engineer and expert in permanent way.

The ten year plan set out to renew the Douglas-Laxey section, followed by Snaefell, financed by an annual grant. Orders were placed with United Steel Mills, Workington, for

Following Government take-over in 1957, the Manx Electric Railway Board decided to give the trams a fresh livery of green and white. It proved so unpopular that the idea was abadoned in 1959 with a return to the traditional M E R style.

200 tons of rail which were delivered to Ramsey along with 3,000 sleepers. Permanent way foreman was Fred Comaish who had worked on the line since 1899. He was due to retire and, with over a hundred men at work on the line, a new post of assistant engineer was created, this being filled by Mr Roy Cannell from the Harbour Board who had previously completed an apprenticeship with the M E R. Estimates for the following year had to be prepared by March and the renewal and operating costs were put at £40,000, well above the intended £25,000, which would mean a subsidy of 50% on every 5 shilling fare. This met with strong opposition and calls for the closure of the Ramsey line. The opposition was narrowly defeated 11-10 in the House of Keys. But the Board was now instructed to run the railway purely as a scenic amenity with no early or late cars and complete closure in winter. Borrowing powers of up to £110,000 were allowed for track renewal with completion of the Laxey section put back to 1965.

The revised summer schedule of eleven return journeys between 10 am and 6 pm was introduced in June 1958 and met with immediate disapproval, so much so that the entire

Board, apart from Mr Kneale, resigned. A new Board was appointed in July with Mr H H Radcliffe MHK as chairman and it was announced that a service of 20 returns would be restored together with a winter service, enabling the Post Office contract to continue. This would be done under the maximum subsidy of £25,000. The Snaefell Summit hotel was refurbished for 1958 although the Bungalow hotel was demolished and replaced by a shelter and toilets, the Board contributing towards the cost. At this time the cars and trailers were supposedly being given a new look by being painted green but the result roused so much opposition from railway enthusiasts that the scheme was abandoned in 1959. Vigorous publicity was rewarded by an increase in passengers with Snaefell patrons increasing from 48,000 in 1953 to 124,000 in 1962. Improvements to the cars were carried out as a result of obtaining equipment from the closure of the Sheffield and Glasgow tramways. But rising costs and wage increases meant that by 1962 over £180,000 had been spent on renewals and operational losses. It is interesting to compare this figure with the £216,000 spent on trying to overcome the fractious nature of the Manx slates of the Marine Drive south of Douglas. A new system of accounting for expenses came into being for 1963-4 whereby the total of operating deficiencies and winter work grants were covered by one figure, and any unspent money had to be returned to the Government treasurer, meaning that good seasonal earnings could not be carried forward for engineering work. The sum allowed for 1963-4 was £39,689 to which was added the cost of building a shelter at Laxey for the Snaefell line and a new station building at Ramsey.

By 1965 the relaying of the section to Laxey was completed and winter work schemes made available to the M E R Board saw the coastal and mountain lines completely weeded and fencing and drainage repaired. The Ramsey line was found to be in remarkably good condition, a tribute to its original construction and sound ballasting. Renewals to the overhead line began in 1958 using traditional round-section trolley wire and phosphor-bronze overhead parts. The poles carrying the wires were completely repainted in dark green and the lineside buildings were similarly smartened, all gateways being painted white. The substations at Ballaglass, Snaefell, Bellevue and Groudle received automatic switch gear to save on manning hours. It was now time to tackle the Snaefell track where the Fell lines were corroding badly at the fishplates and wearing thin on the curves. The Workington steel mills across the sea were prepared to fabricate new Fell rail but at a cost, £145,000, which caused another uproar. An attempt to delete the first instalment of £12,500 from the estimates, with more cries for a road, was defeated in Tynwald. Passenger figures were now averaging 250,000 a year although only 500 a week were using the line in winter. Another commission set up in 1965 to look into public transport proposed closing the Ramsey line but the proposal was not adopted.

Government commitment to the Ramsey line was put to the test when part of the embankment high above Bulgham Bay collapsed in January, 1967. Reconstruction of the embankment started in May and all was back to normal by the middle of July.

Government commitment to the railway was further tested in 1967 where a short section of the embankment wall at Bulgham collapsed in January. Fortunately there were no cars on the section at the time. Further slips occurred in the embankment but services continued with passengers walking along the adjoining closed road from one car to another. A Manchester firm of consultants came to the Island to advise on repairing the embankment and track. Work started in May and wire mesh was embedded in the shale and a lattice of over 100 piles positioned on the rock base, the whole being filled with rubble and concrete. On the surface pre-cast units were laid where the parapet wall had disappeared, these being laid on concrete and forming a base for the track.

Working through the night saw the site safe for passengers able to traverse the area between two special stations which handled 66,000 passengers before the line was fully restored by 10th July. At the end of the year Mr Jack Watson, General Manager and Secretary, retired after 38 years of service to the railway. His successor was Mr Harold Gilmore whose chief assistant was Mr Roy Cannell, with Mr John Gordon becoming traffic superintendent. Mr Gilmore had been apprenticed to the M E R in 1932 gaining experience from house lighting to maintenance of the generating plant. He became a draughtsman with Metropolitan Vickers and worked for the Ministry of Supply before returning to the MER as assistant engineer in 1948.

In August 1970 Mr Gilmore was confronted with a burnt out Snaefell car No 5 which had caught fire on reaching the summit and, with the wind fanning the flames, was totally gutted. With true M E R grit and determination plans were quickly prepared to rebuild the car during the winter and the car was back in service for the following May. While track relaying was progressing on the Snaefell line, the serviceabilty of the cars was beginning to be a cause for concern. At busy times they were a source of embarassment as two or three cars had to be taken out of service. The 80 year old motors were rapidly wearing out and in need of constant attention. When Mr Gilmore reported the position Tynwald, with commendable alacrity, gave authority to

Mr Harold Gilmore, manager, secretary and engineer of the railway, poses beside the restored Snaefell Car No 5 which was badly damaged by fire in 1970. Seated is Mr H. D. Kinnin of Ramsey who undertook the rebuild of the coachwork.

expend up to £150,000 on replacement motors. Where to find them was the problem and London Transport was invited to act as consultants. The search led to Aachen, West Germany, where eleven municipal cars were being disposed off. These cars, built in 1956-57 were of metre gauge and modern design so major modifications would be required to fit the motors into the Snaefell cars. Mr Gilmore, accompanied by Mr John Clucas, chairman of the M E R Board since the death of Mr H H Radcliffe in 1974, set out for Aachen in June 1976, together with two LT engineers, their purpose to examine the cars on offer. The eleven cars were to be sold as a job lot for scrap but negotiations resulted in seven being acquired provided they were removed intact. The seven were shipped to LT works at Acton with one to proceed to Douglas filled with spares. On arrival at Douglas it was discovered that the wrong car had made the journey and was devoid of the spares! Work on adapting the Snaefell cars for the new motors began at Acton while Car No 1 was stripped at Derby Castle and its trucks shipped back to Acton. However, it was found necessary to construct replica trucks to accommodate the motors. These were sent to Laxey car depot where they were installed in No 1 with all the electrical installations and controls fitted ready for commencing service in May 1977. Cars Nos 2 and 3 were revitalised the following year and Cars Nos 4, 5 and 6 during the winter of 1978-9. Instead of the original 4 by 25 hp motors giving a total of 100 hp, each car can now call upon a rating of 244 hp giving them a new lease of life. Rheostatic braking, where the motors are used as dynamos to feed current against the cars' rheostats to produce a retarding effect, is now used. This means that there is little use made of the Fell rail which is retained for use in emergencies.

The Ramsey line finally succumbed in October, 1975, with the loss of the Post Office contract. At the same time the Douglas to Laxey sector was closed for winter service. This was the only time in the railway's history that the entire system was closed. A further heart-searching debate in Tynwald resulted in the decision to keep the Ramsey line closed for the summer of 1976, despite a rearguard action by Mr H C Kerruish, Member for Garff (Laxey and Maughold) and by now Speaker of the House of Keys. He argued that the decision would result in a disproportionate loss to the Laxey and Snaefell lines where rover tickets would be of little value. November 1976 saw a General Election for the House of Keys. The topic of transport was well to the fore at election meetings, not only of the future of the Manx Electric Railway but also of the Isle of Man Steam Railway whose company, after many years of Government assistance, had

MANX
ELECTRIC
RAILWAY

LAXEY - RAMSEY **Adult Return**

ISSUED TO MARK THE RE-OPENING OF THE

LAXEY - RAMSEY Section

Saturday, 25th June, 1977

45p

Issued subject to the Byelaws of the M.E.R. Board

given notice that they were unable to continue. It was quite clear that the Manx public were not prepared to see the demise of the railways and this was reflected in newly elected members. Support for the MER meant that the Ramsey line would reopen for the 1977 season. As regards the steam railway the decision was made to purchase the railway and put its future on a more secure footing so it could continue to play its part as a tourist attraction. The steam railway was to operate under the Manx Electric Railway Board, both electric and steam railways operating under the title of ISLE OF MAN RAILWAYS, though the statutory name of the Board was not changed. Both railways were to be marketed jointly and time tables coordinated. Already, a Tynwald Steering Committee on transport, had recommended that the bus services of Douglas Corporation and Isle of Man Road Services Ltd. be taken over and jointly run as Isle of Man National Transport which was formed in 1976.

The Manx Electric Railway Board lost the services of Mr Harold Gilmore in December 1977 following his retirement, and appointed Mr W Jackson M.C.I.T. as his successor and Chief Executive of Isle of Man Railways. Further changes occurred in 1983 when the Manx Electric Railway Board and National Transport were amalgamated as ISLE OF MAN PASSENGER TRANSPORT BOARD. When a ministerial form of Government was introduced at the end of 1986 the Board system was abolished and transport became part of the DEPARTMENT OF TOURISM AND TRANSPORT under the ministership of Mr Allan Bell MHK. After ten years of service Mr Bill Jackson retired in 1986 and was succeeded by Mr Robert Smith B.A.,M.C.I.T. who became Transport Excutive of the Department. Like his predecessor he has the unique distinction of controlling a transport system involving two electric railways, a steam railway and a fleet of buses.

MAINTENANCE AND PRESERVATION

Responsibility for the maintenance and preservation of the historic steam and electric railways lies in the hands of the railways' Chief Engineer, a position held since 1983 by Mr Maurice Faragher. He and his dedicated staff bring together a wealth of knowledge and a variety of skills which can be applied wherever necessary, whether it be an emergency or a matter of routine maintenance involving the track, electrical supply or the cars themselves. Working within limited resources much graft and ingenuity is required to ensure that the lines are maintained and the cars are ready for another season.

Mr Faragher first had to turn his attention to an incipient slip at the north end of the Bulgham embankment which was causing alarm. To the seaward side of the track a bulge had appeared in the retaining wall indicating that the rock material below was shifting, lubricated by the drainage from the road above. Peg markers on the surface and glass 'tell tales' placed on the face of the embankment overlooking the cliffs below gave precise positions and measurements of the area of the slip. To tackle the problem all loose material was removed, revealing the foundations of the original road before the track was set back in 1903. Holes were then driven down to the bed 15-20 feet below. Old rails were positioned in the holes and concreted in to form a new retaining wall. Resin-bonded reinforcing rods were added to give greater strength. The area was then filled in and concreted, and the wall rebuilt along the original line.

The old power station at Ballaglass built in 1898 has fallen into a ruinous state. It had been sold but the MER retained the portion which housed the substation of 1935. By now the roof was disintegrating with many slates removed and a certain amount of vandalism was also apparent. To rectify matters the substation was removed to the protection of the seaward arch of the nearby Ballagorry bridge.

The original feeder cables from Laxey to the substations at Groudle and Derby Castle have lain underground since 1895 and constant problems of leakage were occurring as the result of corrosion, soil action and damage during track repairs. New cables were out of the question so a new supply was found for Groudle with the co-operation of the Manx Electricity Authority siting a substation on land close to the old battery house. Thus the Groudle substation was supplied with 11 Kv which passes through a composite

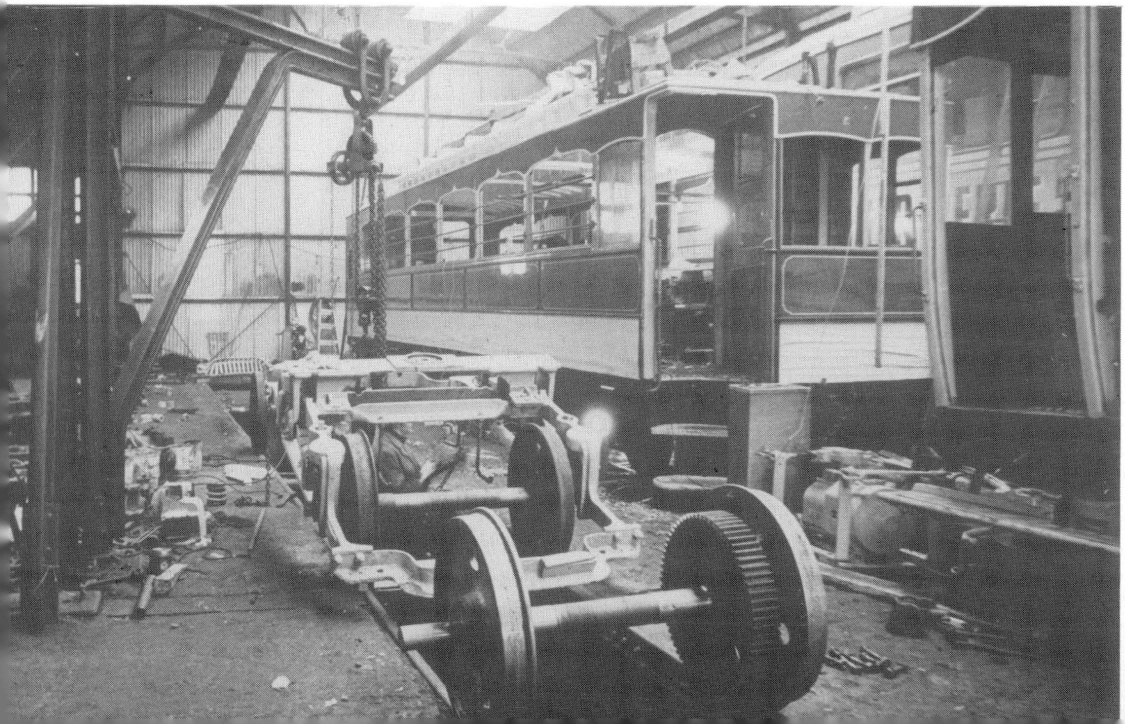

A typical scene in the workshop at Derby Castle. During the period 1977-79 the Snaefell cars, one of which is shown here, had their original motors and controls replaced by more modern ones obtained from Aachen. All the electrical installation work was carried out at Derby Castle. In the foreground motors have been removed from the bogie of a coastal car for inspection.

transformer with fuse switch gear, supplied by G E C Alsthom. The rectifier then provides the 550 volts DC required by the cars. At Derby Castle the emergency supply is now in use as a temporary measure, this coming from the MEA substation at the top of Summerhill in Blackberry Lane. This supplies 3.3 Kv which is transformed and rectified at the Derby Castle substation. The overhead wires are renewed when and where necessary, depending on the wear from the trolley wheels. BICC Callender cables are ordered in quarter mile lengths, an average of four such lengths being required each year. The total number of poles covering the coastal route is 904, every fifth one being numbered from Derby Castle with the last one in Ramsey station. They are spaced every 45 yards with closer spacing on the curves. Very few of the original ones are still in place and today about ten are replaced each year, using galvanised poles from British Steel.

Where a replacement is necessary the new pole is inserted adjacent to the old pole to a depth of 6 feet. When the arms have been transferred, the old pole is then cut down from ground level. On the Snaefell line there are 179 poles, the higher ones being of wood because they are more capable of standing up to the high winds and not so liable to earth in icy conditions. Normally the overhead wires are removed from the top quarter of a mile (poles 164-179) and tied to the Fell rail. Occasionally, however, they are left in order to take up supplies to the radar station built at the summit by the Air Ministry in 1950. Experience has shown that the weight of ice forming on the wires is so great that they have snapped, especially on the exposed north shoulder of the mountain. Down at Laxey, the Snaefell car shed is being doubled in width, work commencing during the winter of 1989-90. This will give additional space so that all winter maintenance can be undertaken at Laxey rather than by the previous custom of transferring the cars to Derby Castle on special bogies. The new depot will have updated facilities to maintain the sophisticated Aachen motors, the manuals for which have been translated from the German! The new block contains an amenities room and supervisor's office.The winter of 1990-91 also saw the 180 foot Ballure bridge receive considerable attention. The timber decking has been replaced and the metal work sand-blasted in readiness for priming, undercoating and glossing. Over 80 gallons of superior paint was used in the renovation. In 1988 an additional guard rail was placed along the outer rails, this being purely a precaution in case of a derailment.

continued on page 36

Maintenance of the permanent way is part of the winter work. In 1983 attention was given to slipping at the north end of the Bulgham section. Here old rails are being positioned vertically to form part of the retaining wall to prevent future damage to the track.

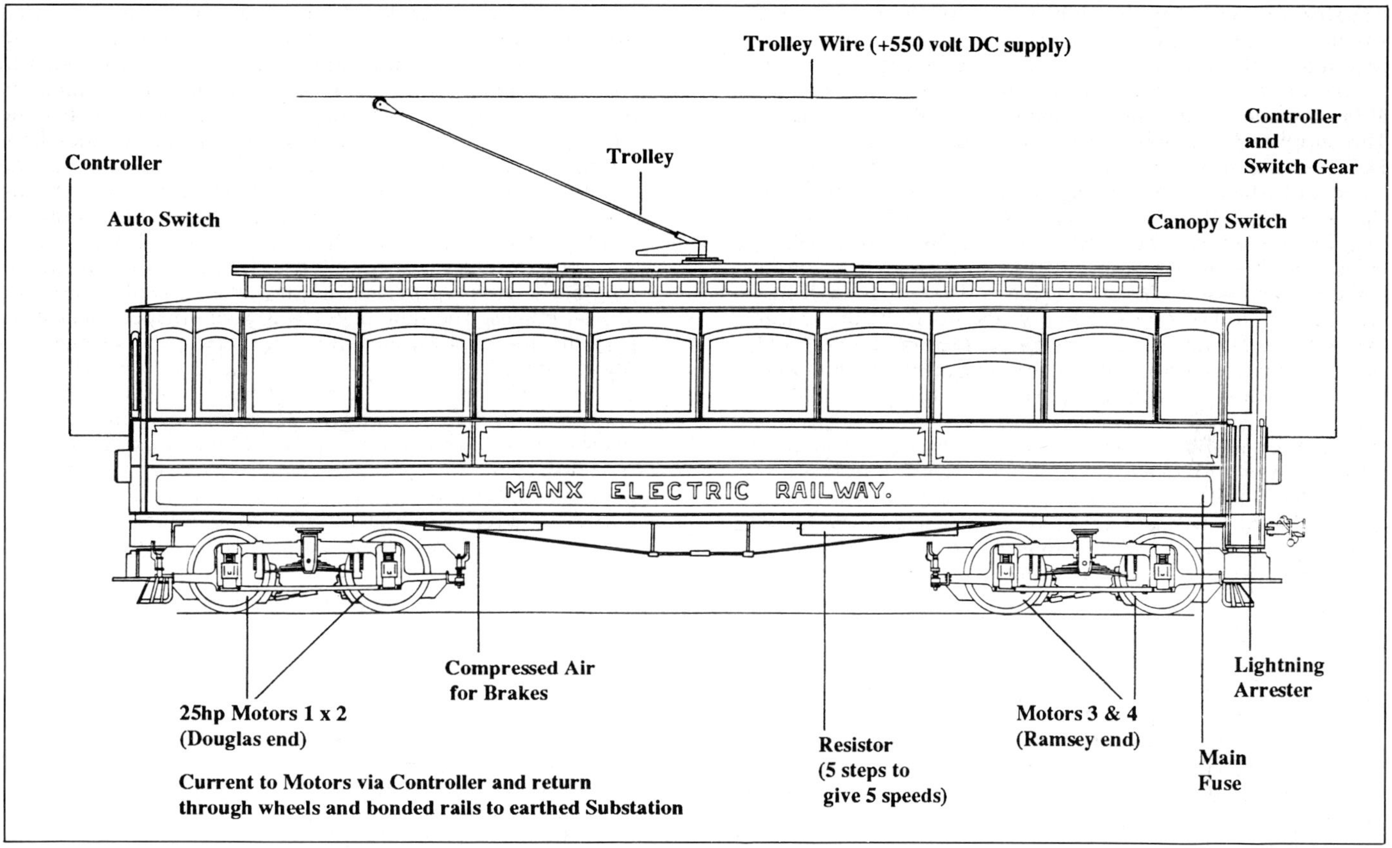

DETAILS OF CAR ELECTRICS

The TROLLEY receives a 550 volt DC supply from the OVERHEAD TROLLEY WIRE. This is led first to the AUTOMATIC SWITCH which trips should the supply become overloaded. From here the supply is led along the top of the car to the CANOPY SWITCH, another safety point. The current then passes to the MAIN FUSE BOX which is linked to the LIGHTNING ARRESTER and earthed for the return through wheels and rails. Power enters the motorman CONTROLLERS which are connected from either end and determine the amount of current passing through the RESISTOR to the four MOTORS. Under the car the electrically-driven COMPRESSOR supplies the air brakes and a governor controls pressure from a maximum of 100 lbs to a minimum of 75 lbs per square inch. (The ratchet cars have manually operated brakes). All cars have a sanding device which can be operated by foot to provide additional wheel adhesion. During the winter of 1990-91 Car No. 20 was fitted at the Ramsey end with the pressurised system as used by the Aachen cars.

Maintenance and overhaul of the coastal cars takes place at the Derby Castle Depot where some of the original buildings and equipment remain in use. To the seaward side are the car sheds of 1894-96 with seven roads on which the regular cars and trailers are stored for the winter. The two sheds are separated by a modern amenities block from the 1893 car shed, stores and workshop area. The car shed, or fitters' shop, has three roads known as 'hospital,' 'middle,' and 'stores.' The hospital road is immediately adjacent to the maintenance bay. From here an entrance leads to the machine shop, which was originally the boiler and engine house, and now contains the transformer and substation. Belt-driven machines for sawing, planing and wheel pressing are still in use while lathes and drills are of modern design. Overlooking the machines is a timely reminder of the early days, this being the original clock still working and marked' Isle of Man Tramways and Electric Power Company.' In front of the machine house the shed of 1923-24 is now occupied by the joiners shop next to which is the paint shop, once the goods shop and still with its bay. In charge of the Depot is Rolling Stock Supervisor Daryl Gribbin whose staff consists of two fitters, a blacksmith, painter, joiner (with apprentice), an electrician and four general handymen.

Apart from routine maintenance there is usually at least one car undergoing a major overhaul. The chosen car is jacked up in the paint shop and bogies and equipment removed to the fitters' shop. The four motors are removed from the bogies and split to inspect the armatures and coils. Rewinds are undertaken in the workshop from coils provided by specialist electrical engineering firms. Length of life of the armatures varies considerably. For example, in Car No. 16 motors 1 and 3 have recently had rewinds while motor 2 was last rewound in 1937, number 4 motor still using the original armature of 1899. Number 1 motor in Car No.26 of 1904 was found to have a burnt out coil and was recoiled in 1990, the original armatures of the other three motors still being in good condition. Each winter normally sees two rewinds completed. Many of the white metal bearings of the motors, which required daily oiling, have been replaced since 1978-79 with grease-packed roller bearings. Controllers, rheostats and the vital resistance are thoroughly checked. Overhauls also see the brake rigging stripped and then put through the Smithy fire to remove any crystalline build up, new parts being fitted if necessary. Wheels of the early tyre type are being replaced by new solid ones. Back in the paint shop the bogies are repainted before being attached to the underframe. Car bodies are repainted in Middle Mason Red and White, traditional M E R colours, with wood panels varnished and beading picked out in light brown.

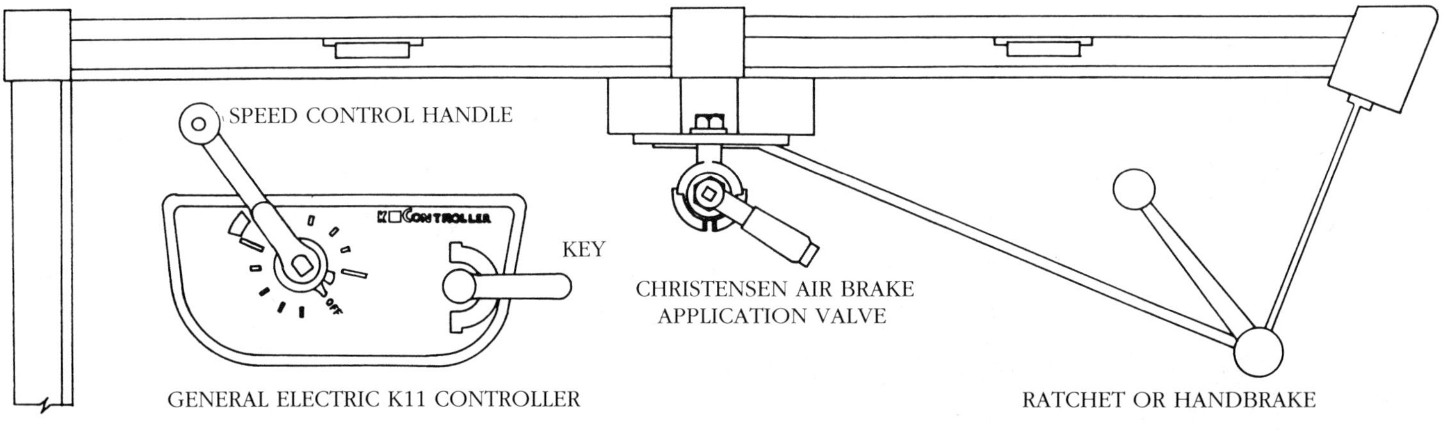

Diagram of car controls.

TO BE A MOTORMAN

Although each of the trams has only two basic controls, the controller to make the tram move and a brake for stopping, there is much more to being a trained motorman than a knowledge of these controls. Amongst the permanent staff the M E R has a number of motormen who man the regular service cars while the additional 'specials' required in summer are generally manned by seasonal staff.

The railway has a thorough training programme for would-be motormen which not only teaches him how to move and stop the tram, but also gives instruction on how the tram works, the various components, the different types of tram in use, emergency procedures, and thorough familiarisation of the working of the railway. Following a demonstration run, where every movement is explained, a number of runs between Douglas and Laxey is made, and when the trainee is capable of driving the car supervised, he is transferred to a service car for further training along the entire length of line. After a number of weeks, and when deemed competent, a thorough practical and oral examination is undertaken.

During the 1904 re-equipment of the cars, it was decided to standardise on the General Electric K11 controller, as delivered on the 1898-9 cars. All controllers remain in use but have been modified to K12 circuitry over the years. The GE controller has two handles, a speed control and a key. The key fits onto the right hand side of the controller and is turned forwards or backwards depending on the direction of travel. For safety reasons it cannot be moved unless it and the speed control are in the OFF position. The speed control is on the left hand side of the controller. As it is rotated through a number of steps or 'points,' resistance in the circuits are cut out and the car increases speed.

There are five series points and four parallel points. At the first point, the motors are connected in two pairs, in series with each other with the whole of the resistance in circuit. Points 2 - 4 reduce the resistance, until on 'five points' all the resistance is cut out. On the first parallel point, all motors are now connected to the power, with the resistance in circuit again, being reduced on points 7 and 8, until on 'nine points' all resistance is cut out and the car has maximum power. A motorman must not remain on any resistance point longer than is necessary as power fed to the resistance is burnt off as heat, the running points being top series and top parallel. Power must be switched off cleanly with a single, clean motion. Care must be taken when notching up, taking into consideration gradient, load etc.

As well as the normal handbrake, all cars, except 14,15,17,18 and 28-31, have compressed air brakes. They are applied by a hand controlled application valve situated to the right of the controller. Air under pressure is bled off from the reservoir by turning the handle to the right, pressure is held in the middle or running position, and bled off to the atmosphere by turning the handle to the left. On descending a gradient, the motorman can be seen to continually work the brake valve, bleeding off air, and releasing in order to keep a constant braking effect under the varying conditions. On stopping a car, air is slowly bled off as the car slows to avoid a wheel lock, and the brake is then firmly re-applied when the car has come to rest. The application valve on cars 21 and 22 differs from the others. The desired braking effect is achieved by holding the handle in any position, the further to the right the greater the braking. Air is released by moving the handle to the left hand side.

In an emergency, and only then, the reversing key on the controller can be moved into the position opposite to the direction of travel, in order to use the motors as an emergency brake, but causes great stress and strain to the electrical equipment. Each car is fitted with a foot operated warning gong but in those cars with air brakes, the gong has been superceded by a distinctive air whistle. The larger pedal to the right of the whistle is a sand pedal, used by the motorman in the event of wheel skid to deposit sand on the running rails. Wheel skid is most likely when the rails are damp rather than soaking wet.

THE FIRE AND RESTORATION OF CAR 22

On Saturday, 29th September 1990, Car 22 with 57 trailer were working the 2.00 pm ex-Derby Castle scheduled service. On board was a group of visitors from Germany. Whilst on the ascent from Lhen Coan to Baldromma, the motorman began to experience adhesion problems on the damp and greasy rails past Eskadale. In an attempt to overcome the difficulty, the resistance box mounted beneath the body of the tram became subject to abnormal temperatures. The car came to a stop at pole 157 and the effect of the wood charring caused the passenger compartment to fill with smoke and the passengers alighted. The motorman radioed Derby Castle Station and Mr Paul Ogden, Assistant Operations Superintendent, despatched Car 20 as a 'back up.' Chief Engineer Mr Maurice Faragher arrived on the scene to find that a fire extinguisher had been applied to the resistance box and surrounding areas which now appeared to be safe. The trailer was uncoupled and the car was able to move forwards which indicated that the resistance had not 'open circuited' and everything was intact. The passengers were transferred to Car 20, and 22 with trailer returned to Derby Castle.

At the Depot the trailer was returned to its shed and Car 22 to the bottom shed of the workshop area for further observation. Wisps of smoke were appearing and a dry powder extinguisher was emptied on the charred area. By 6.00 pm. as staff were going home, the car was checked again with no apparent sign of fire. A further inspection was made at 9.15 pm and no sign of smoke or flame was discovered. It was not until 7.30 the following evening, Sunday, that the auto dial fire alarm in the Douglas Fire Station Control signalled a fire to which appliances were sent immediately. A member of the public also raised the alarm having seen smoke coming from the roof of the shed. The fire was intense but brought under control amidst clouds of smoke and steam. When it was possible to inspect the car it was found to be very badly damaged with the floor and side panelling completely burnt out. The resistance box was lying on the floor still connected by the burnt out cables. Despite all the action that had been taken, the cause of the fire seems to have been caused by an ember lying between the original wood floor and plywood sheeting which had been fitted during Car 22's recent overhaul. Draughts through the shed had fanned the ember causing it to ignite undetected.

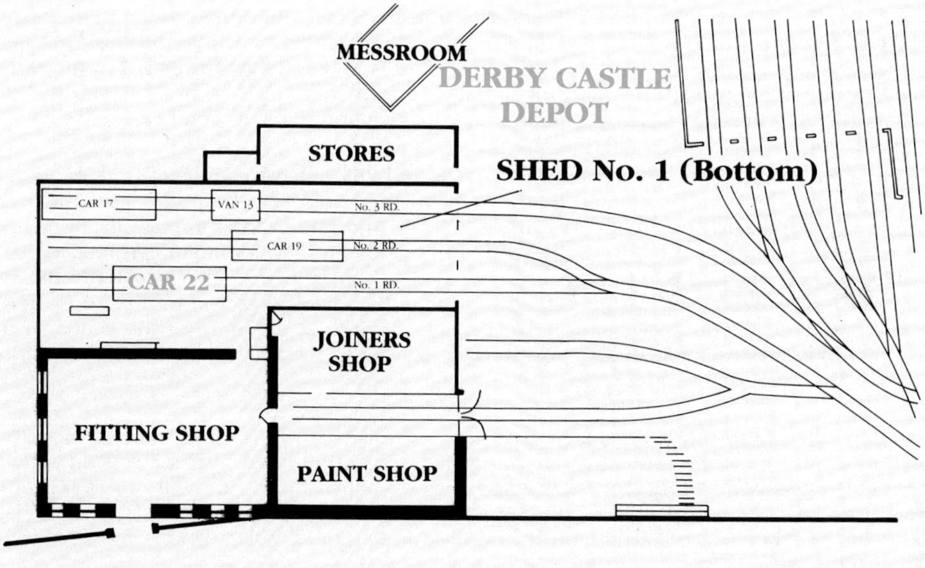

Plan of Derby Castle Depot showing position of Car 22 when it was severely damaged by fire on the night of Sunday, 30th September, 1990.

Within a fortnight the Chief Engineer had submitted a report about the incident and suggesting the cause of action to be taken pending the restoration. All vehicles and equipment are heavily insured by Government. To begin with instructions were issued for a 'heat shield' to be fitted to all the fleet, the shield consisting of gypsum-based non-combustible board sandwiched between two sheets of steel. In addition, the resistance boxes are to be lowered to provide a four inch gap between box and shield. Also called into question is the use and effectiveness of the sanding equipment, standard on all motor cars. Sand delivery pipes are being checked and modified, if necessary. The original wire reinforced canvas piping has long been replaced by solid piping which are now having flexible tubing added to ensure that the sand is delivered directly on to the rail. The system is operated by a foot pedal by the motorman with sand being applied between the wheels nearest the controller. To ensure that all motormen, many of whom are 'summer only,' are familiar with the application of sand in 'bad rail' conditions, more intensive instruction will be given. Regulations already state that motormen should check sanding equipment before taking a car from the Depot yard.

While the frame and trucks survived the fire with little damage, the coach and carriage work requires a complete rebuild. All ironwork is being replaced to original design by Porter Engineers of Carlisle. Items include the seating supports with M E R motif, clerestory roof braces, corner brackets, sliding door gear and floor plates. The major part of the reconstruction involves the complicated woodwork. With no original plans available a new set has been prepared. They are a work of art in themselves, having been created by Mr Eric Cleator, a former Government Clerk of Works who has been appointed Project Supervisor. Put out to tender, the work has been awarded to McArds of Port Erin. They are working to detailed drawings for the floor plan, bulkheads, doors, jointing and panelling. The sectional drawings of posts, rails, mouldings etc. are exact full size and can be used directly to make moulding patterns. All types of joints are in traditional form and only materials of the highest standard are being used. Types of wood include long grained English oak, Pitch pine, Western Red Cedar, long grained teak and teak faced marine plywood, the latter for cladding. All brass fittings are also being replaced as are doors and light fittings, the latter having crystal glass shades. As a touch of modernity, Car 22, one of the 'winter saloons' of 1899, and its trailer are being equipped with a public address system for use on special excursions in the future.

The charred remains of Car 22 which is now being faithfully restored to its original design.

MANX ELECTRIC RAILWAY

The Derby Castle terminus is at the northern end of Douglas Promenade and is served by the Horse Tramway and frequent bus services on routes 24 & 26 as well as the promenade service 30 which connects with the steam railway station.

The horse tram depot at Derby Castle houses a fine collection of horse and cable tramway relics, including the superbly restored cable tram No. 72/3. A return trip to Ramsey or Snaefell Summit takes at least three hours and tickets must be purchased from the small wooden booking office which, erected in 1897, is the only surviving IOMTEP Co building at Derby Castle.

A regular timetable is operated, but in summer specials or extra cars run between the timetabled cars, so that a frequent service is operated.

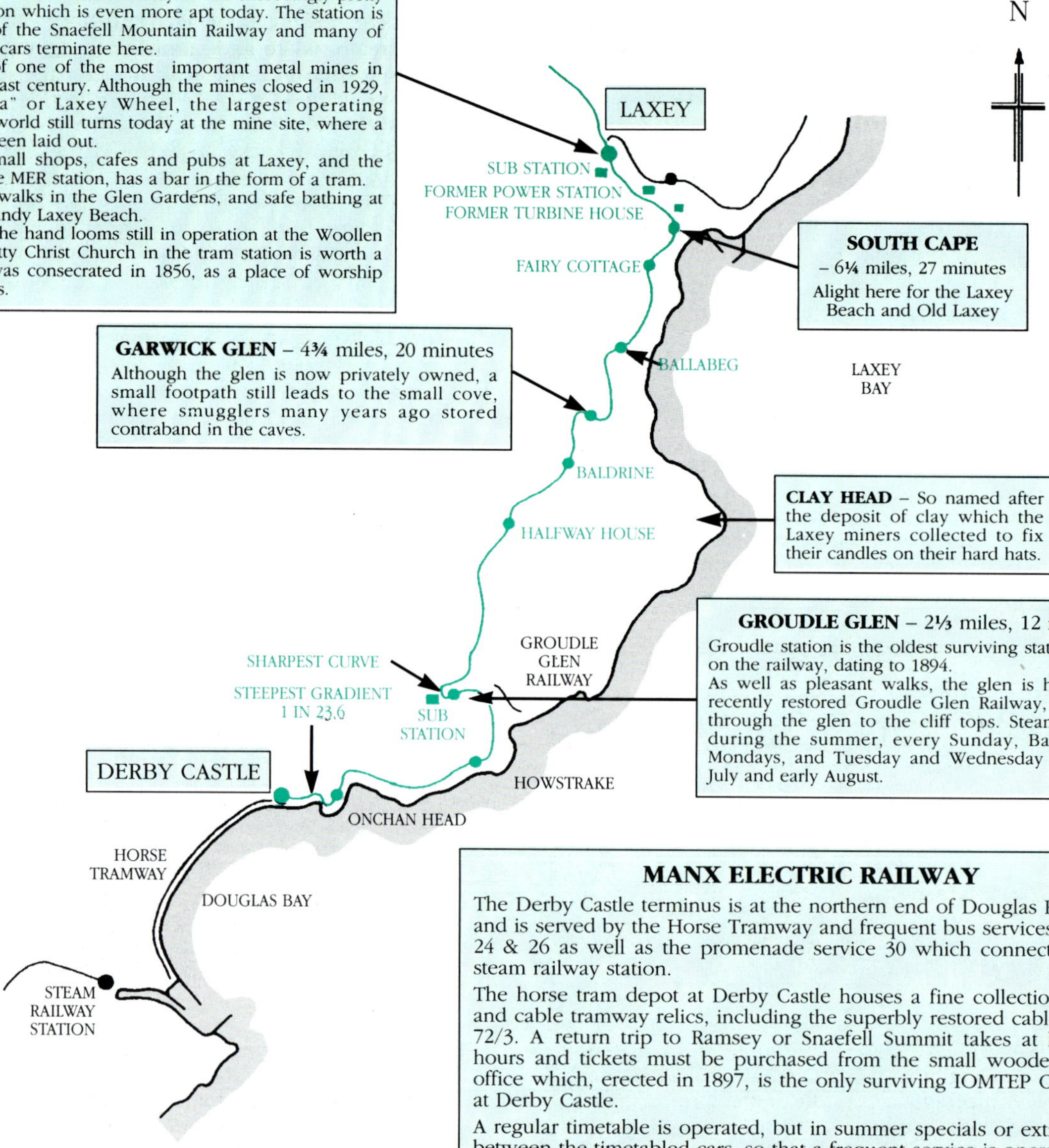

LAXEY STATION – 30 minutes, 7 miles

An old guide book once described Laxey as "an exceedingly pretty station", a description which is even more apt today. The station is the starting point of the Snaefell Mountain Railway and many of the extra or special cars terminate here.
Laxey was home of one of the most important metal mines in Britain, during the last century. Although the mines closed in 1929, the "Lady Isabella" or Laxey Wheel, the largest operating waterwheel in the world still turns today at the mine site, where a "mining trail" had been laid out.
There are many small shops, cafes and pubs at Laxey, and the Mines Tavern, in the MER station, has a bar in the form of a tram.
There are pleasant walks in the Glen Gardens, and safe bathing at the sheltered and sandy Laxey Beach.
Visitors can watch the hand looms still in operation at the Woollen Mills whilst the pretty Christ Church in the tram station is worth a visit. The Church was consecrated in 1856, as a place of worship for the Laxey miners.

SOUTH CAPE – 6¼ miles, 27 minutes

Alight here for the Laxey Beach and Old Laxey

GARWICK GLEN – 4¾ miles, 20 minutes

Although the glen is now privately owned, a small footpath still leads to the small cove, where smugglers many years ago stored contraband in the caves.

CLAY HEAD – So named after the deposit of clay which the Laxey miners collected to fix their candles on their hard hats.

GROUDLE GLEN – 2⅓ miles, 12 minutes

Groudle station is the oldest surviving station building on the railway, dating to 1894.
As well as pleasant walks, the glen is home of the recently restored Groudle Glen Railway, which runs through the glen to the cliff tops. Steam trains run during the summer, every Sunday, Bank Holiday Mondays, and Tuesday and Wednesday evenings in July and early August.

THE ROLLING STOCK

Apart from the short-lived class 10-13 of 1895, and those cars lost in the 1930 Laxey Depot fire, all the cars of the Manx Electric Railway remained in existence until 1990 when Car 22 was badly damaged by fire. The promoters of the Douglas - Groudle line turned to G F Milnes and Co, of Birkenhead for the rolling stock. The arrival of class 10-13 brought the first transverse seating which allowed better viewing from the cars. Open crossbench cars followed in several batches, whilst Cars 19-22 saw a new level of luxury, intended for all year round service. The last motor cars to be delivered, Nos. 32 and 33, arrived in 1906.

The newly formed Manx Electric Railway Company inherited rolling stock that was already becoming outdated so a modernisation programme was embarked upon with Brush type D equal wheel bogies. Later cars were delivered with Brill type 27 trucks. Various modifications have been carried out to control gear and electrical equipment over the years, but the original car bodies remain in use and have seen very little alteration.

The livery of the tramcars has always been a combination of red, cream, white and varnished teak. When delivered Cars 1-3 were finished with teak upper panels and cream lower panels, lettered DOUGLAS AND LAXEY COAST ELECTRIC TRAMWAY, whilst Nos 4-9 differed in being lettered DOUGLAS AND LAXEY ELECTRIC TRAMWAY. Cars 10-13 were finished in teak completely and lettered as 4-9. Nos 19-22 were painted in a similar style to 4-9 but lettered DOUGLAS, LAXEY AND RAMSEY ELECTRIC TRAMWAY, the TRAMWAY later becoming RAILWAY. The open cars were at first finished with varnished brown uprights, which later gave way to white.

THE MANX ELECTRIC RAILWAY Co. Ltd. title appeared from about 1904, with the rocker panel painted red with a white border, and intricate lining out of the panel. Post Second World War economies saw the title reduced to M E R with no linings. Following nationalisation, a vivid green livery was

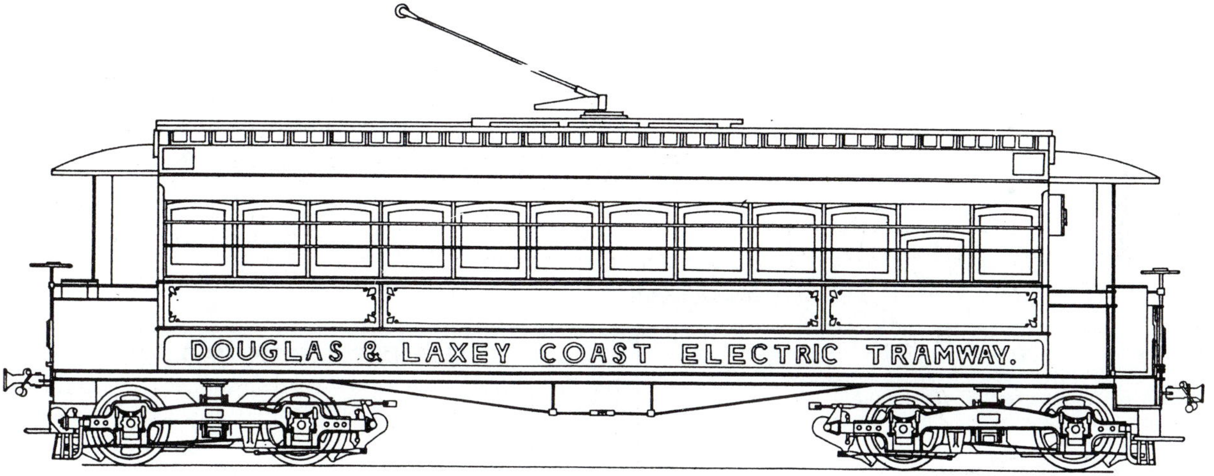

CARS 1 to 3

Built 1893 by G F Milnes and Co. Unvestibuled door, seating for 34 people on longitudinal seating. Original Mather and Platt electrical equipment and Milnes plate frame bogies replaced in 1903 with Brush type D equal wheel bogies, each bogie having two 25 hp SEHC motors. Control gear replaced by General Electric controllers. Air brakes fitted at the same time. Car 3 was destroyed in the Laxey Depot fire.

Car 1 was traditionally used as the winter PW car and Car 2 as the wire car. Car 1 restored as near as possible to 1893 condition in 1979 and Car 2 in 1981. Car 1 is now the oldest electric tramcar still operating regularly in passenger service in the world, a fact recorded in the Guinness Book of Records. Car 2 is just a few days younger.

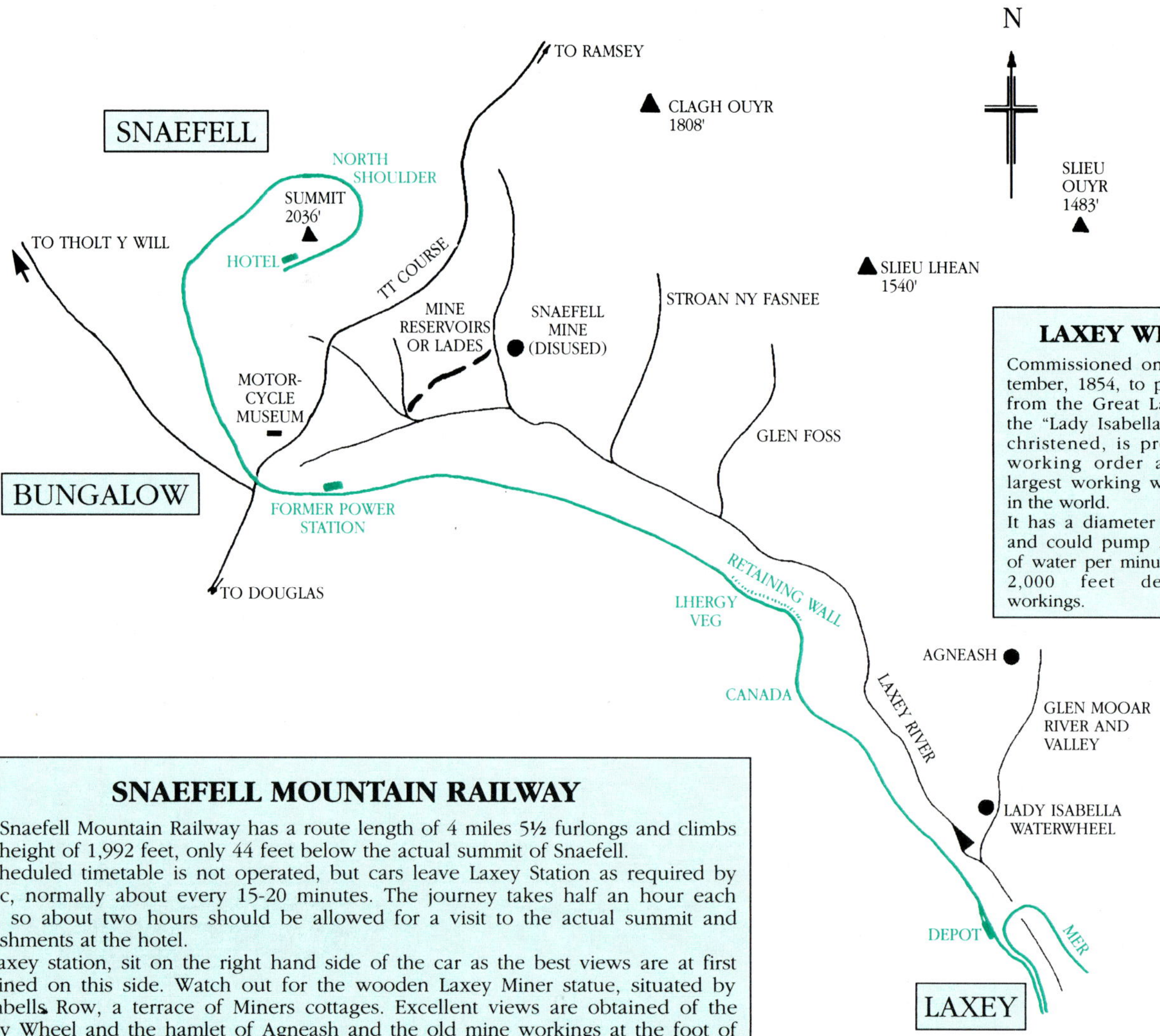

LAXEY WHEEL

Commissioned on 27th September, 1854, to pump water from the Great Laxey Mine, the "Lady Isabella" as it was christened, is preserved in working order and is the largest working water wheel in the world.
It has a diameter of 72ft 6in and could pump 250 gallons of water per minute from the 2,000 feet deep mine workings.

SNAEFELL MOUNTAIN RAILWAY

The Snaefell Mountain Railway has a route length of 4 miles 5½ furlongs and climbs to a height of 1,992 feet, only 44 feet below the actual summit of Snaefell.
A scheduled timetable is not operated, but cars leave Laxey Station as required by traffic, normally about every 15-20 minutes. The journey takes half an hour each way, so about two hours should be allowed for a visit to the actual summit and refreshments at the hotel.
At Laxey station, sit on the right hand side of the car as the best views are at first obtained on this side. Watch out for the wooden Laxey Miner statue, situated by Dumbells Row, a terrace of Miners cottages. Excellent views are obtained of the Laxey Wheel and the hamlet of Agneash and the old mine workings at the foot of Snaefell are clearly visible. This was the scene of the Island's worst mining disaster in 1897, when 21 miners were killed.
Above the Bungalow, the best views are obtained on the left hand side. As the car climbs and spirals around the mountain, Eire and Northern Ireland can be seen to the West, Scotland to the North and England to the East.

adopted and some cars so painted. The livery was totally out of character and so unpopular that the scheme soon reverted to the traditional image. In 1978, the lettering was changed from MANX ELECTRIC RAILWAY to ISLE OF MAN RAILWAYS, with plastic stick-on letters, again totally out of keeping with the historic nature of the rolling stock. From 1979, certain cars have been repainted in former historic liveries, whilst others have been repainted in styles similar to these, but not an historic reproduction. No 6 appeared in 1982 lettered ISLE OF MAN PASSENGER TRANSPORT whilst more recent repaints have seen a reversion to MANX ELECTRIC RAILWAY.

All motor cars are fitted with a Hughes Patent coupler, invented by Albert Hughes of G F Milnes and Co., for use with steam tramway trailers. This extremely effective coupler also acts as a buffer. Although in theory it is possible to connect any car with any trailer, in practice certain cars are only paired to certain trailers. For example, Cars 25 and 26 are seen with trailers 55 and 56 while Cars 32 and 33 go with trailers 62 and 61. The 'ratchet' cars are normally only coupled to 'bulkhead' trailers. The differing body heights of cars and trailers entails the use of specially cranked coupling bar for each pair.

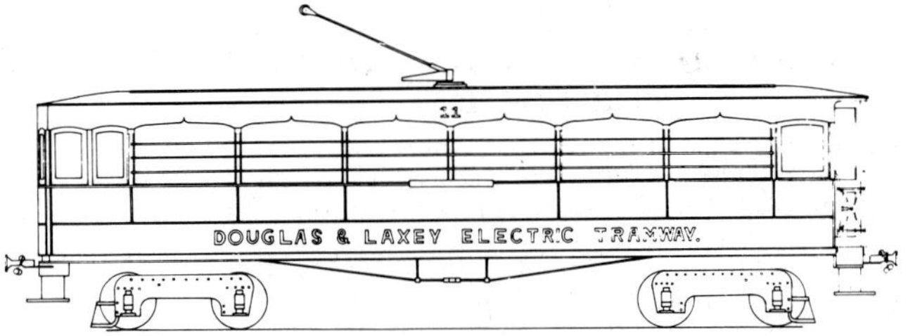

CARS 10 to 13

Built 1895 by G F Milnes and Co. Vestibuled saloon, bodies almost identical to Snaefell cars. Seated 46 on transverse seating. Less expensively finished than the earlier cars, with unglazed saloon windows. All withdrawn from passenger service in 1902. No. 12 rebuilt as a motored cattle car in 1903 and a second as a 'goods motor' in 1904. Other two cars stored until 1918 and then rebuilt as freight trailers. The sole survivor, goods trailer 26, formerly Car 10, survived in store until 1978 when preserved in the Railway Museum. Hopefully it will one day be restored to its original 1895 condition.

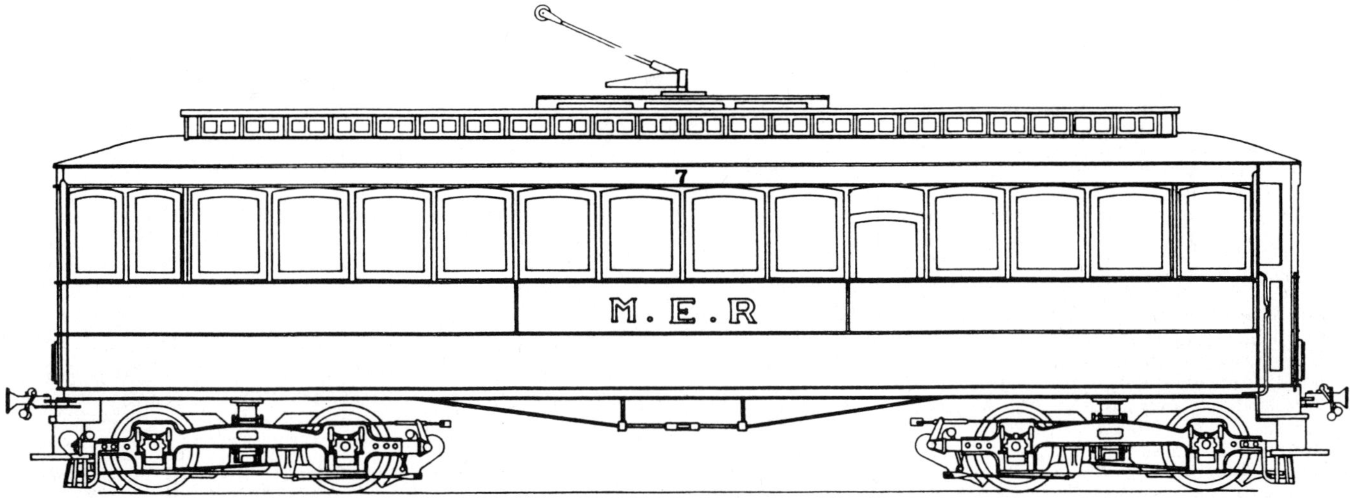

CARS 4 to 9

Built 1894 by G F Milnes and Co. Vestibuled saloon, seating 32 people on longitudinal seating. Car 4 exchanged trucks with Car 16 in 1899. Original Mather and Platt electrical equipment and Milnes plate frame bogies on Nos 5-9 replaced in 1903 with Bush type D equal wheel bogies, each bogie having two 25 hp SEHC motors. Control gear replaced by General Electric controllers. Air brakes fitted at same time. Cars 4 and 8 destroyed in Laxey Depot fire. Car 5 received transverse seating in 1932. Known as 'Tunnel Cars,' 5, 6, 7 and 9 remain in service.

ROYAL RAMSEY – CAPITAL CITY OF THE NORTH

Ramsey grew from a tiny fishing village to town status in 1865. Attractions include the Mooragh Park and Boating Lake north of the picturesque harbour and connected by the swingbridge. There is good shopping in the narrow streets and numerous cafes and tea rooms. The lifeboat house and 2,330 feet long Queens Pier, opened in 1886, is still open to the public. To the north, on the Andreas Road, is the Grove Rural Life Museum, a superb example of a Victorian Country House, preserved by the Manx Museum and National Trust.

THE RAMSEY ELECTRIC RAILWAY MUSEUM

The Museum is situated in the former tram depot just south of the station. The three main exhibits comprise of Locomotive 23, mounted on spare trailer bogies as a static exhibit, bogie freight trailer 26 converted from passenger car 10 in 1918 and saloon trailer 59, used by King Edward VII and Queen Alexandra in 1902. 59 may at times be absent if required in service.

The museum also contains large amounts of photographs, tickets, posters and handbills, as well as examples of Permanent way equipment, an overhead pole and controllers, etc.

Recent additions includes surplus Douglas Corporation horse cars Nos. 11, built in 1886, No. 47 of 1911 and convertible all weather car 49 of 1935.

The petrol locomotive and small toastrack trailer which used to run along the Queens Pier are also exhibited.

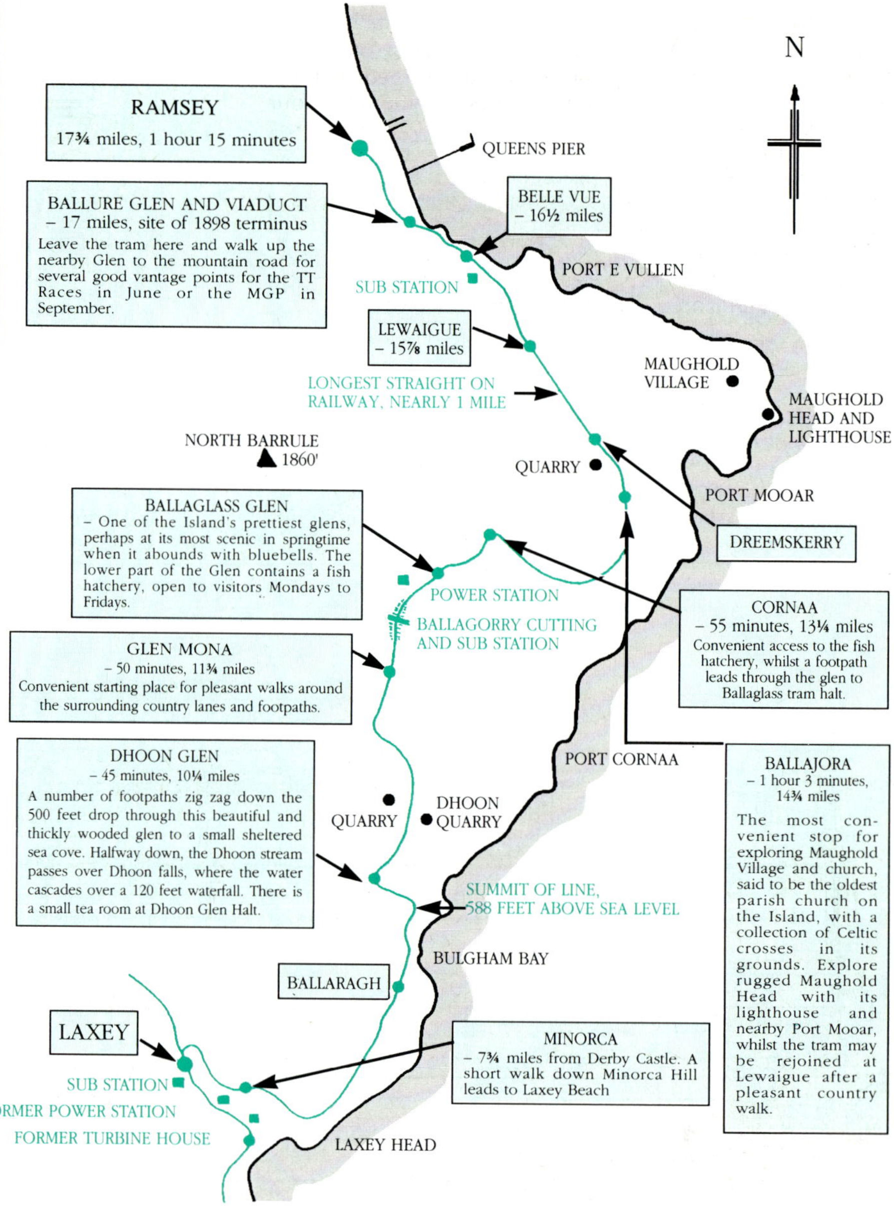

CARS 14 to 18

Built 1898 by G F Milnes and Co. Open crossbench cars with roller shutters, seating 56. Nine sets of Milnes plate frame bogies each with two 20 hp motors were obtained in 1898, five of the sets being placed on these cars and the other four held back for winter saloons 19-22. The other four open crossbench cars obtained in the same batch became trailers. Car 16, now with the trucks of Car 4, re-equipped in 1903 with Brush type D bogies and air brakes. Nos.14, 15, 17 and 18 retain their handbrakes only, known as 'Ratchets' or 'ECC Bogies' due to their motor type. Car 16 remains in regular use, Car 18 used periodically. Car 14 serviceable while Cars 15 and 17 remain stored, electrical equipment removed.

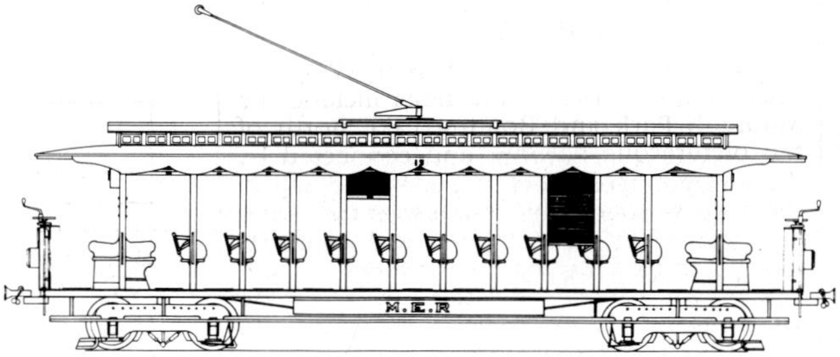

CARS 19 to 22

Built 1899 by G F Milnes and Co. 'Winter Saloons' seating 48 on transverse seating. Given the four unused sets of 1898 equipment. From 1904, the class received the trucks, equipment and air brakes from Nos 28-31, receiving Brill type 27 trucks. The largest cars on the railway, they became the mainstay of M E R's all year round timetabled service, covering the greatest mileage. Class remained intact until 1990 when Car 22 was destroyed by fire. Replica bodywork subsequently by McArds of Port Erin, and electrical and mechanical work rebuild at Derby Castle Depot.

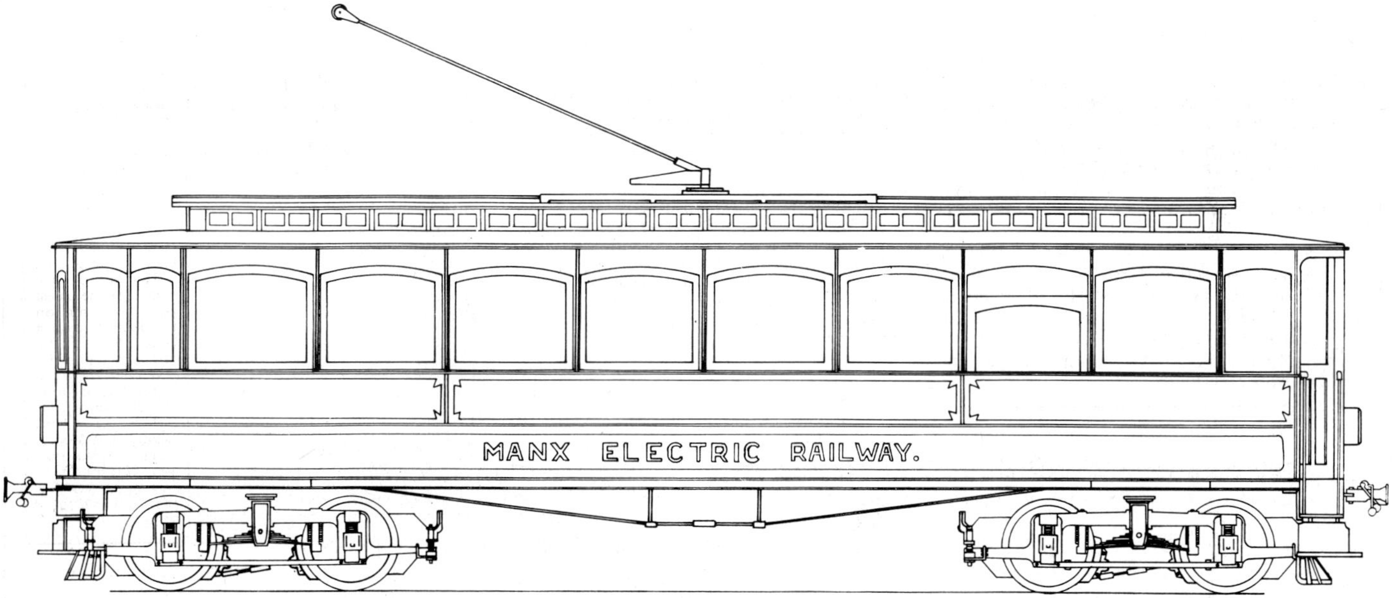

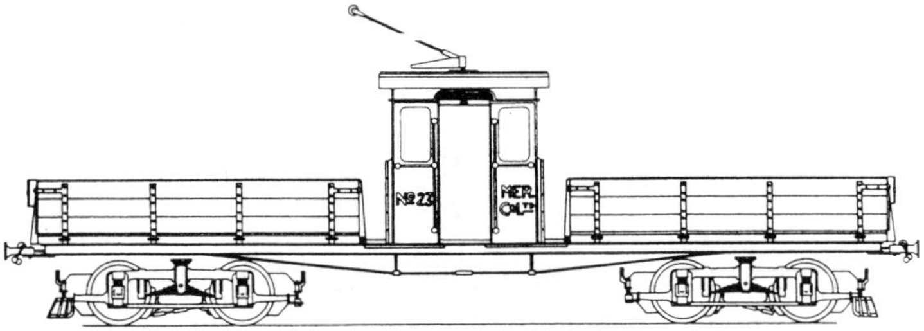

LOCOMOTIVE 23

Built in 1900 by IOMTEP Co. at Derby Castle to the design of Frank Edmundson. A centre type cab locomotive with sloping ends, which borrowed equipment from Car 17 each winter. Designed for use on heavy stone traffic. Severely damaged in a collision at Bulgham in 1914, stored until 1925 and rebuilt, the centre cab being mounted on a new underframe between two six ton wagon bodies. Borrowed equipment from Car 33. Disused after 1944 and stored at Laxey until 1978 when cosmetically restored for the Ramsey Museum. Fully restored to working order in 1983-4 for Vintage Transport events but is now once again a static exhibit at Ramsey.

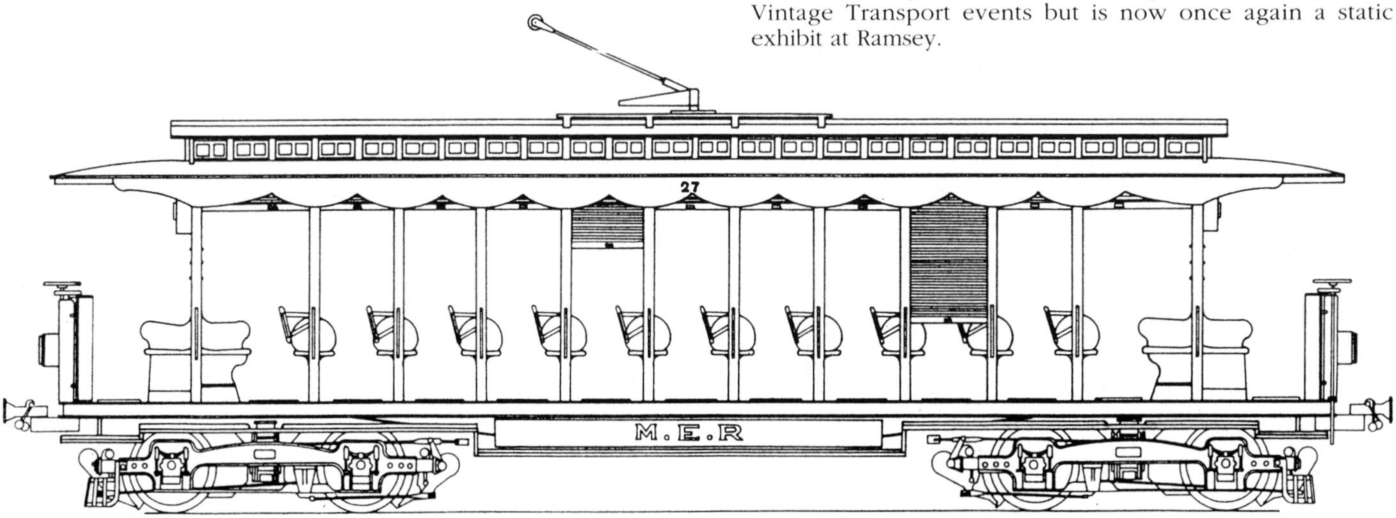

CARS 24 to 27

Purchased as identical to Cars 14-18 but became unmotored trailers Nos 40-43. Motorised by M E R Co. in 1903 with Brush type D Bogies and renumbered Nos 24-27 forming a class with No 16 and known as 'paddleboxes' due to the steps in their running boards to accommodate the Brush bogies. 24 was lost in the Laxey Depot fire while 25-27 are in regular seasonal use.

CARS 28 to 31

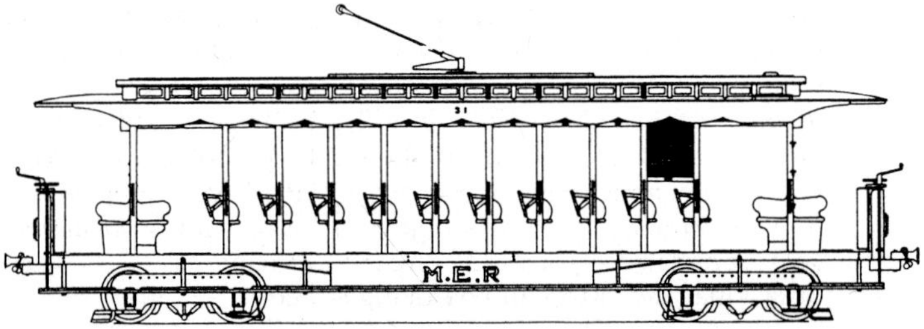

Built by Electric Railway and Tramway Carriage Works Ltd., Preston, in 1904, G F Milnes and Co. at this time facing closure. Open crossbench cars with roller shutters seating 56. Each car had two Brill type 27 trucks with two outside hung 25 hp motors. As previously detailed, trucks and equipment including air brakes exchanged with Nos 19-22 in 1904, due to their excellent performance. Now known as 'Ratchets' due to their reliance on hand brakes only. All cars remain but see almost no use. Car 31 serviceable, 29 possibly a runner, 28 and 30 stored withdrawn and minus electrical equipment.

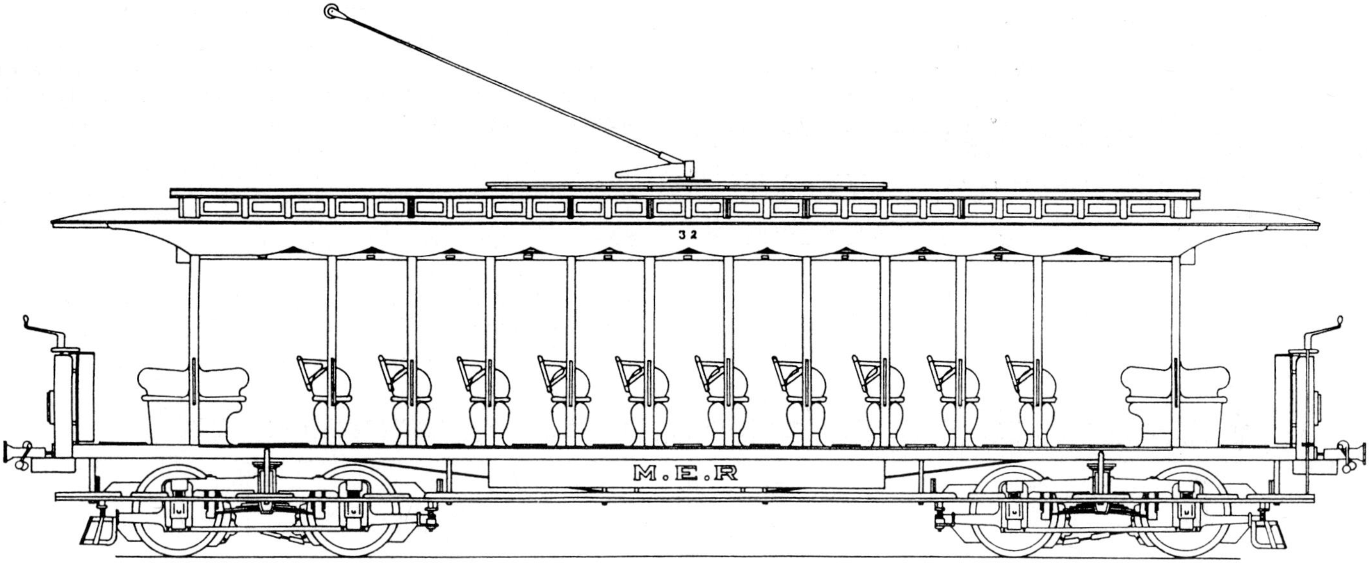

CARS 32 and 33

Built by United Electric Car Company, successors to ERTC Works. Open crossbench cars with roller shutters seating 56, almost identical to Cars 28-31. Brill type 27Cx trucks each fitted with two GE 27½ hp motors, the 110 hp total making these two cars the most powerful on the line. Both remain in active service, almost unaltered from the time of construction.

TRAILERS

Although the motor cars are numbered in approximately the order of construction, some of the trailer cars have been renumbered several times, as the fleet of motor cars expanded. All trailers are fitted with an extremely effective emergency brake. A chain attached to a ratchet on the brake rod linkage is secured to a hook on the motor car underframe. The chain contains a weak link so that in the unlikely event of the main coupling fracturing, the chain tightens, pulls on the trailer brakes which are locked by the ratchet and snaps, preventing further damage.

49-54. Built by G F Milnes and Co in 1893. Basically lengthened horse trams on light frame bogies. Seat 44. As built were totally open but received canvas roofs in 1894 and then wooden roofs in 1904. Wooden bulkheads added some time later. As built were numbered 11-16. All trailers exist, but 52 was converted for PW work about 1947. In 1987 No 51 was rebuilt into its wooden roof form, with dash panels and renumbered 13. Of the remainder only 49 sees occasional use, 50,53 and 54 being stored.

34-39. Built 1894 by G F Milnes and Co. Seats 44 and built with wooden bulkheads and roofs. Probably numbered 17 to 22 when built. 34,35,38 and 39 destroyed in Laxey Depot fire in 1930. 37 still sees use, 36 stored. Known as 'Bulkhead Trailers,' although description is now also applied to Nos 49-54 and 60.

Trailer 59. Special saloon car for Directors and guests' use. Built 1895 by G F Milnes and Co. Smallest piece of passenger stock on the railway, seats 18. As built it was mounted on four wheel trunnion gear but by 1900 was mounted on a spare pair of Milnes plate frame bogies. In August 1902 59 carried King Edward VII and Queen Alexandra and has since been known as the 'Royal Trailer.' Still sees use occasionally, especially on private hire.

Trailer 60. Built in 1896 by G F Milnes and Co. Seats 44 and same construction as 34-39. Survived the Laxey fire and still sees use.

44 to 48. Built in 1899 by G F Milnes and Co. Seats 44, crossbench with roller shutters. Although of same dimensions as earlier trailers, of a more substantial construction, with clerestory roof. 44 lost in Laxey fire, others see regular intensive seasonal use.

40 to 43 Built by G F Milnes and Co. Seats 44, open crossbench with roller shutters and clerestory roof. 40 and 41 lost in Laxey fire, 42 and 43 still in regular use.

55 and 56. Built by Electric Railway and Tramway Carriage Works in 1906 as part of same order as Nos 28-31 and 57-58. Essentially similar to the Milnes products, seating 44, with roller shutters, but a finer finish and more substantial product. Mounted on Brill 27 trailer trucks. In regular use.

57 and 58. Built 1904 by ERTCW, unvestibuled saloon trailer, seating 32 on transverse seating. Designed for winter service, complete with air brakes. With their beautifully finished interiors and Brill 27 trucks, the pair offer a superb ride and see occasional use, especially in early and late season.

40, 41 and 44 (11) Built 1930 by English Electric to replace stock destroyed in Laxey Depot fire. Seats 44, roller shutters and mounted on salvaged Milnes plate frame bogies from burnt 1894 trailers. Still in regular use.

GOODS STOCK

The goods stock has always been numbered separately from the passenger stock. Items remaining are as follows:

No. 1 Built 1894, six ton open wagon.

Nos. 3 and 4 Built 1894-5. Four-wheeled van with end platforms.

Nos. 7 and 8. Built 1897-8, six ton open wagons.

Nos. 11 and 12. Built 1898-9. Four-wheel van, 11 with platforms removed, 12 with platforms and tower platform added in 1977.

Nos. 13 and 14. Small vans, no platforms, built 1904.

No. 16. Large mail van, with end platforms removed.

No. 21 Bogie PW wagon known as 'Dreadnought' fitted with two Challenger lifting cranes in 1977 for loading rails.

There is also an unnumbered tower wagon constructed on a former wagon chassis.

Written by Gordon N. Kniveton and Andrew A. Scarffe

With acknowledgement to staff of Isle of Man Railways

Technical drawings and colour photography by Andrew Scarffe

Jointly published by The Manx Experience, 10 Tromode Close, Douglas,

and Isle of Man Railways, Strathallan Crescent, Douglas, Isle of Man.

Printed by Print Centres Ltd., Braddan, Isle of Man.

(Back cover) Snaefell Mountain Car 6 at Lhergy Veg on the ascent to the Bungalow and summit.